D0792668

BALANCING ACTS

RENEWALS 458-4574

THE BALANCED BUDGET DEBATE SERIES

This report is the first in a series commissioned by the Twentieth Century Fund to examine the potential impacts of a federal balanced budget amendment.

WITHDRAWN
UTSA LIBRARIES

THE BALANCED BUDGET DEBATE

Richard Briffault

BALANCING ACTS

The Reality Behind State Balanced Budget Requirements

A TWENTIETH CENTURY FUND REPORT

1996 ◆ The Twentieth Century Fund Press ◆ New York

*Library
University of Texas
at San Antonio

The Twentieth Century Fund sponsors and supervises timely analyses of economic policy, foreign affairs, and domestic political issues. Not-for-profit and nonpartisan, the Fund was founded in 1919 and endowed by Edward A. Filene.

BOARD OF TRUSTEES OF THE TWENTIETH CENTURY FUND

Morris B. Abram
H. Brandt Ayers
Peter A. A. Berle
Alan Brinkley
José A. Cabranes
Joseph A. Califano, Jr.
Alexander Morgan Capron
Hodding Carter III
Edward E. David, Jr.
Brewster C. Denny
Charles V. Hamilton
August Heckscher
Matina S. Horner

Lewis B. Kaden
James A. Leach
Richard C. Leone
P. Michael Pitfield
Richard Ravitch
Arthur M. Schlesinger, Jr.
Harvey I. Sloane, M.D.
Theodore C. Sorensen
James Tobin
David B. Truman
Shirley Williams
William Julius Wilson

Richard C. Leone, *President*

Library of Congress Cataloging-in-Publication Data

Briffault, Richard.
    Balancing acts : the reality behind state balanced budget requirements / Richard Briffault.
        p.   cm. -- (The balanced budget debate series)
    "A Twentieth Century Fund Report."
    Includes bibliographical references and index.
    ISBN 0-87078-394-7
    1. Budget--United States--States.   2. Budget--Law and legislation--United States--States.   3. Finance, Public--United States--States.
    I. Twentieth Century Fund.   II. Title.   III. Series.
HJ2053.A1B69   1996
339.5'0973--dc20   96-21838
                                                                        CIP

Cover design and illustration: Claude Goodwin
Manufactured in the United States of America.

Copyright © 1996 by the Twentieth Century Fund, Inc. All rights reserved. No part of this publication may be reproduced, stored in a retrieval system, or transmitted, in any form or by any means, electronic, mechanical, photocopying, recording, or otherwise, without the prior written permission of the Twentieth Century Fund, Inc.

FOREWORD

The doctrine of devolution so beloved by today's Congress proclaims that states will succeed where the federal government fails. Welfare, Medicaid, job training, environmental protection, and even school lunches, according to believers, will become more effective and efficient when the states are unshackled from federal supervision.

One of the ways in which state governments are said to outshine their federal counterpart is financial management. The states, it is widely maintained, balance their budgets year in and year out. Indeed, almost all states have some sort of constitutional or statutory provision that refers to budget balancing. If only such discipline could be enforced on the deficit-ridden federal government, most of the people who hawk devolution assert, the nation would receive a plethora of benefits. Hence, the march toward amending the U.S. Constitution to mandate a balanced federal budget.

But are the states really the laboratories of fiscal prudence that their admirers claim? To answer that question, the Twentieth Century Fund asked Columbia University law professor Richard Briffault to examine in detail why and how states strive to balance their budgets. His work is enormously valuable because it reveals the main lesson that can be drawn from the state experience is that a federal balanced budget amendment would be more harmful than beneficial.

For one thing, all states with balanced budget requirements—whether constitutional or statutory—also have capital budgets (a special category of overall budgets that includes spending on long-term projects) that are not subject to those constraints. States use capital budgets when they borrow for investment in roads, bridges, college buildings, and many other projects that will provide benefits for years to come. Without capital budgets, states subject to balanced budget requirements could not spend more than they collect in taxes in any given year. Instead, just as families borrow to pay for homes and college tuitions and companies take out loans to invest in new plants and equipment, states accumulate debt to finance investments that promise rewards extending beyond the current year. But the federal budget is not divided into capital and current spending, and none of the proposed balanced budget amendments provides for a capital budget. Thus, unlike the states, the federal government would be constrained from borrowing to support long-term projects.

Federal government spending also plays a vastly more important role in the domestic economy than total state spending does. All but the most radical conservatives agree that using budget allocations and tax revenues to smooth the rough spots in the business cycle—say, in a recession, when tax receipts fall and spending for unemployment insurance and other programs rises—is good for the economy. Those automatic responses offset the recessionary forces and speed recovery. They are among the reasons that economic downturns have been less severe since World War II. Indeed, the insistence on balancing the budget during the 1930s is generally regarded as having made the Great Depression worse. The countercyclical features of the current system matter, and giving them up will impose real costs, particularly on working men and women. Remember, income lost when government cannot fight a recession is lost forever.

The balanced budget bandwagon derives much of its horsepower from the belief that we can achieve good government—a government we can trust—only by having less government. But maybe, deep down, it is ourselves we don't trust. Is the balanced budget amendment attractive because we hope it will protect us from our own unwillingness to make hard choices, such as electing people with the guts to tell us no when we ask for services or to insist that we accept the taxes needed to pay for them?

Bear in mind that the national debt nearly quadrupled from 1981 to 1992, a period that began when Ronald Reagan convinced the public that if tax rates were cut, especially for the well off, the budget would be balanced through growth alone. In short, lots of gain with no pain. Today's problems spring, in part, from the feeling voters have that they allowed themselves to be hoodwinked by Reagan's notions. Over the eleven-year span from 1981 to 1992, the annual deficit increased from $79 billion to more than $290 billion. As a percentage of gross domestic product, the gross federal debt ballooned from about a third to more than two-thirds, and it remains at about 70 percent of GDP today.

These numbers are disturbing, but the federal government has demonstrated that it can reverse the trend without the straitjacket of a balanced budget amendment. In fact, the 1993 deficit reduction package left the United States with the lowest deficit as a percentage of GDP among industrialized nations. Currently, fiscal conservatives make up a clear congressional majority, demonstrating anew that democracy, functioning normally, can change in the direction of budgetary policy. Amending the Constitution to fight the national debt is a deceptively simple "solution," but in the end it will only make difficult economic decisions worse. Instead, we should sensibly debate how to restructure the nation's budget and tax policies in ways that will contribute to long-run growth and more economic equity.

On behalf of the Trustees of the Fund, I want to thank Richard Briffault for this paper, the first in a series of publications the Fund will release analyzing the potential impact of a balanced budget amendment. Forthcoming papers will examine how particular states might be affected by the proposed change.

RICHARD C. LEONE, PRESIDENT
The Twentieth Century Fund
May 1996

CONTENTS

INTRODUCTION

We need a constitutional amendment requiring a balanced budget. It is something that 49 States already require. . . . [There is] no reason the Federal government should be any different.

President Ronald Reagan
March 1, 1985[1]

We desperately need the power of a constitutional amendment to help us balance the budget. Over 70% of the American people want such an amendment. They want the Federal Government to have what 44 State governments already have . . . discipline.

President Ronald Reagan
August 12, 1987[2]

Forty-four of our States have some kind of a constitutional requirement for a balanced budget. It's time for the Federal Government to follow their lead.

President George Bush
June 10, 1992[3]

For most of the past two decades, the federal budget deficit has been a major focus of public concern. The deficit ballooned at the beginning of the Reagan administration and has persisted at historically high levels ever since. To solve the deficit problem, many officials, commentators, and ordinary citizens have urged that the Constitution be amended to mandate a balanced budget.

Indeed, both the Senate and the House of Representatives have, in different years, voted to submit a balanced budget amendment to the states for ratification. The House of Representatives overwhelmingly passed a balanced budget amendment early in 1995. That proposal failed in the Senate by just two votes , with majority leader Bob Dole indicating he would bring it back for another vote[4] at some point during the current Congress.[5]

As the statements of Presidents Reagan and Bush demonstrate, balanced budget amendment advocates frequently cite the experience of the states in making the case for a federal balanced budget amendment. The argument from the state experience relies on the following syllogism: (i) states have constitutional balanced budget requirements; (ii) states achieve balanced budgets; ergo, (iii) the constitutional requirements cause state budgets to be balanced.[6] For amendment proponents, the states' experience demonstrates that American governments can function with constitutional balanced budget requirements and that an amendment to the U.S. Constitution will provide the federal government with the same fiscal discipline it now lacks but that the states enjoy.[7]

This paper analyses the lessons of the states' experience with constitutional balanced budget requirements for a federal amendment. The paper is concerned not with the wisdom, as a policy matter, of cutting the federal budget but rather with the role of constitutional requirements in achieving budgetary balance. The fiscal provisions of state constitutions do have consequences, but, as will be seen, their impact on the structure, function, and performance of state governments is probably not what balanced budget amendment advocates anticipate or desire.

The first part of this paper examines the two premises of the syllogism: whether states are required by their constitutions to balance their budgets and to what extent they actually do so. The middle sections address the interaction of balanced budget requirements with other aspects of state government and state constitutions. The final chapter returns to the last leg of the syllogism to consider the contribution of balanced budget constitutional provisions toward states' achieving fiscal balance.

Chapter 1 assesses what state constitutions actually require with respect to budgetary balance. Despite sweeping assertions that forty-four or forty-nine out of fifty state constitutions require balanced budgets, the number of constitutions that directly address budgetary balance is more like thirty-six, and many of those do not actually require that the entire state budget be balanced or that it be balanced without borrowing. Capital funds and a multiplicity of special funds often are not considered a part of the state budget subject to the balanced budget requirement.

Chapter 2 turns to whether and how states actually balance their budgets. This is a surprisingly difficult question. States have discretion in designing their budget structures, and many do not adhere to generally accepted accounting principles (GAAP) in their budget methods.[8] It appears that, on their own terms, most states balance their budgets most of the time whether or not they are required by their constitutions to do so. Indeed, of the ten states that took steps to eliminate deficits that emerged during the 1992 fiscal year, four had no legal requirements of year-end balance and one—Vermont—had no constitutional balanced budget requirement at all. On the other hand, some states, including those with balanced budget requirements, run deficits some of the time.

Some states manage to achieve balance technically through a range of clever gimmicks, fiscal tricks, and budgetary sleights of hand. A state may juggle cash and accrual accounting methods so that revenues are counted in the year they accrue but expenditures are deferred to the year cash is paid out. Other gambits include deferring payments to vendors, selling off assets, or underfunding pension plans. Beyond accounting tricks, states in fiscal extremis can reduce their contributions to local governments or demand greater local fiscal responsibility for shared governmental functions. Conversely, states have become adept at manipulating federal aid programs to increase Washington's support for state budgets. A significant portion of the explosion in the growth of the Medicaid program in the late 1980s and early 1990s, for example, was a result of the states' skill in taking advantage of federal law and shifting traditional state public health costs to the federal government.

Chapter 3 considers how balanced budget requirements have affected the political balance of power within state governments. These requirements, in tandem with other state practices, have tended to strengthen the executive branch and weaken legislatures. Governors have been given broad authority to shape state budgets and reduce legislatively authorized spending during the fiscal year—powers far greater than those wielded by the president over the federal budget. Constitutional balanced budget amendments also have implications for the third branch of government—the courts. If a constitution requires a balanced budget, then the rules of the fiscal process become matters of constitutional law. In fact, there has been relatively little judicial enforcement of state balanced budget requirements, which raises a significant question concerning the importance of the balanced budget amendments in constraining states. Nevertheless, litigation over balanced budget rules and other fiscal provisions of state constitutions occurs, thereby giving state courts a far greater role in the law and politics of public finance than U.S. courts currently play.

Chapter 4 devotes detailed consideration to state constitutional restrictions on debt. States' debt limits deserve special attention for three reasons. First, many advocates of a federal amendment rely on state debt restrictions rather than balanced budget provisions when they tabulate the number of states subject to balanced budget amendments. Thus, the debt restrictions are directly relevant to an appraisal of the state balanced budget experience. Second, state courts play a major role in determining the actual impact of state constitutional debt restrictions on state fiscal behavior. Their interpretations demonstrate how court decisions come to influence fiscal policy when fiscal issues are placed within state constitutions.

Third, state debt limitations—or, rather, the techniques for their evasion—have contributed to shaping the intricate patterns of state finance and the complex structure of many state governments. With the approval of state courts, state legislatures have avoided debt limitations through the development of new borrowing devices that create obligations considered not to be "debt" and through the creation of new, quasi-autonomous agencies that are not treated as part of the state government bound by the debt limits. Indeed, these mechanisms have enabled state legislatures to avoid balanced budget requirements as well as debt limits. The history of state debt limitations thus shows that constitutional restrictions on state fiscal behavior can affect public finance practices in perverse ways, stimulating the growth of avoidance mechanisms that actually increase government costs, insulate agencies from political accountability to the voters, and fragment government.

Finally, Chapter 5 considers the importance of state balanced budget provisions in the attainment of fiscal balance. Most states' adherence to sound fiscal practices may be as attributable to the structure of our federal system and the demands of the credit market as to formal state constitutional requirements. The states lack the fiscal and monetary tools and the tax base of the federal government. States can neither print money nor close their borders to prevent residents and businesses from fleeing to other jurisdictions to avoid high levels of state taxation. In order to borrow, a state must demonstrate to potential lenders its capacity to repay its debts. If it persistently ran a significant deficit, its creditworthiness would be undermined. It would have to pay a substantial penalty in terms of higher interest rates or, ultimately, risk loss of access to capital markets. States are like households or businesses. They balance their budgets not necessarily because their constitutions require it—after all, households and businesses are not subject to constitutional requirements—but because the marketplace demands it. Legal requirements no doubt affect state fiscal practices. But the bond market and the interstate competition for tax base, not state constitutions, probably do the real work of imposing fiscal discipline on the states.

Chapter 1

DO STATE CONSTITUTIONS ACTUALLY REQUIRE BALANCED BUDGETS?

A careful reading of state constitutions demonstrates that the states are far less constrained by their constitutions to balance their budgets than proponents of a federal balanced budget generally assume. First, in a significant number of states there is no constitutional—as opposed to statutory—balanced budget requirement. Second, state constitutional balanced budget provisions often fail to preclude deficits. Third, many state constitutional balanced budget rules apply to less than the entire state budget.

THE DIFFERENCE BETWEEN CONSTITUTIONAL AND STATUTORY REQUIREMENTS

Proponents of a federal balanced budget amendment contend that the special constraint of a constitutional provision is needed to compel a balanced budget. In their view, a statute requiring a balanced budget lacks the necessary force since a statute can be readily changed or superseded. Only a constitutional amendment, so the argument goes, can bind Congresses and presidents actually to bring the budget into balance. Yet, ironically, although amendment advocates are careful to distinguish between the feeble effect of a statute and the coercive force of a constitutional provision at the federal level, they often fail to be as precise in differentiating between constitutions and statutes at the state level. Instead, they blur the two together when they contend that virtually all—forty-nine out of fifty states—are required by their constitutions to have balanced budgets.

In fact, a close examination of state constitutions reveals that only thirty-six make any reference to the balancing of budgets. Of the other fourteen—Alaska, Arkansas, Indiana, Iowa, Maine, Minnesota, Mississippi, Nebraska, New Hampshire, New Mexico, North Dakota, Vermont, Washington, and Wyoming—all but one (Vermont) have *statutory* balanced budget requirements. The tabulation of states with and without constitutional balanced budget provisions is more than a little imprecise. Even balanced budget proponents have used varying numbers in making the argument to look to the experience of the states. At different times President Reagan referred to forty, forty-four, and forty-nine states with constitutional balanced budget requirements. This uncertainty may be attributable to the nature of constitutional law. Constitutional provisions take on their meaning as a result of many years of interpretation by elected officials and courts. A balanced budget rule may result from a judicial reading of constitutional language that does not refer to the state budget.[1] Conversely, the effect of a balanced budget provision can be eroded by case law or administrative practices.

Former governor John Sununu of New Hampshire captured this uncertainty when he acknowledged that "in most of the states you will find the constitutional requirements rather ambiguous." Indeed, as chair of the National Governors Association he once argued to Congress that his state is subject to a balanced budget requirement because of a "pair of phrases within the constitution, one of which admonishes us to frugality."[2] Similarly, some commentators contend that in Arkansas a balanced budget requirement has been "generated by case law from constitutional language that does not appear to address the issue."[3]

Several of the states without constitutional balanced budget provisions nonetheless do have constitutional limitations on debt, such as restrictions on how much the state may borrow or requirements that the state obtain voter approval in a referendum before it may incur debt. Some amendment proponents treat these as constitutional balanced budget requirements. But, as will be discussed in a later chapter, state debt limits are often evaded and thus do not function effectively as balanced budget mandates. Moreover, some states whose constitutions limit long-term debt permit short-term debt, which can allow a state to carry over a deficit from one fiscal period into the next.

In short, the number of states actually subject to a constitutional balanced budget requirement is more like three-quarters rather than all save one. Of course, three-quarters is still a substantial figure, but not all of the state constitutional provisions actually require states to balance their budgets in the sense of having revenues equal or exceed expenditures during a fiscal period (either a fiscal year, or, for states with biennial budgeting, a two-year period). A close reading of state constitutions reveals that some balanced budget provisions do not preclude states from running year-end deficits or from borrowing to obtain the revenues necessary to pay for current expenditures.

What Do State Constitutional Balanced Budget Provisions Require?

It is often difficult to determine what a state's constitutional balanced budget provision actually stipulates. As the National Conference of State Legislatures has noted, "constitutional and statutory provisions requiring balanced budgets are often unclear, making it impossible to count the different kinds of requirements with precision."[4] Similarly, the National Association of State Budget Officers (NASBO) has cautioned that "rather than addressing specific processes and procedures to insure balanced budgets, they tend to be generally worded constitutional provisions that are subject to varying interpretations."[5]

Some constitutions require no more than that the governor submit a plan for a balanced budget to the state legislature. The Massachusetts constitution, for example, states simply that the governor shall submit "a budget which shall contain a statement of all proposed expenditures of the commonwealth for the fiscal year, including those already authorized by law, and of all taxes, revenues, loans, and other means by which such expenditures shall be defrayed."[6] That's it. There is no requirement that the legislature pass a balanced budget. And even the governor's budget may be balanced by the use of borrowing as well as by tax dollars. Similarly, the constitutions of California, Michigan, and New York require only that the governor submit a balanced budget to the legislature, not that the legislature actually enact one.[7]

According to NASBO, only thirty-one state constitutions actually require their legislatures to pass balanced budgets.[8] These requirements are often generally worded and typically fail to provide any enforcement mechanism. The Florida constitution states: "Provision shall be made by law for raising sufficient value to defray the expenses of the state for each fiscal period."[9] The Colorado constitution declares: "The General Assembly shall provide by law for an annual tax sufficient, with other resources, to defray the estimated expenses of the state government for each fiscal year."[10] These are directives to states to raise sufficient funds to cover their costs, but they do not compel a reduction in expenditures should revenues fall short.

Indeed, many state constitutions refer to "estimated expenditures" and "anticipated revenues" at the start of the fiscal period rather than actual balance at the end. According to the Connecticut constitution, for example, "the amount of general budget expenditures authorized for any fiscal year shall not exceed the estimated amount of revenue for such fiscal year."[11] A state that is poor at budget estimation may run deficits while still satisfying its constitution's balance requirement. Thus, although Idaho requires its legislature to pass a balanced budget, NASBO found that "there are no sanctions, and in recent years the legislature has overappropriated its general account revenue estimates for the coming year."[12]

Moreover, at least twenty constitutions, and possibly more, either permit states to carry deficits over into the next fiscal year or enable state governments to borrow money to finance a budget deficit. Language in the constitution may expressly contemplate carrying forward a deficit. The Wisconsin constitution, for example, affirms that the legislature "shall provide for an annual tax sufficient to defray the estimated expenses of the state for each year," but, in the next breath, it allows that "whenever the expenses of any year shall exceed the income, the legislature shall provide for levying a tax *for the ensuing year*, sufficient, with other sources of income, to pay the deficiency as well as the estimated expenses of such ensuing year."[13] Similarly, the Nevada constitution indicates that one year's deficit can be paid off in the "ensuing year or two years."[14]

In a 1992 survey, NASBO found that thirteen states are permitted to carry deficits over into the next fiscal period. With one or perhaps two exceptions, these are ordinarily considered to be "balanced budget" states.[15] In addition, in seven other states[16] the sole legal authority for the restriction on deficit carryovers is statutory, not constitutional. A 1993 survey of state budget officials by the United States General Accounting Office came up with a similar count, although there is some difference in the GAO and NASBO's determinations of which states have no requirement of year-end balance. According to the GAO study, budget officers in ten states,[17] most of which are balanced budget states, said they were not subject to requirements of year-end balance. Budget officers in another eleven states[18] said that carrying over a deficit or borrowing to finance one are allowed if necessary. The GAO survey received no response from one state,[19] nor did it distinguish between constitutional and statutory requirements of budget balance. Thus, the number of constitutions interpreted by state officials to require year-end balance or to forbid either carryovers or borrowing to cover a deficit may be somewhat less than thirty.

WHAT PORTION OF STATE BUDGETS IS COVERED?

Even if a state is required by its constitution to balance its budget in the strong sense that it may not carry a deficit over into the next fiscal period, that requirement may not apply to all of the state's funds. State finances are extraordinarily complex. Although all states have general funds that are used to pay for most operating expenses, most states have also established a host of special funds—forty-two states have created one or more distinct capital funds to finance the acquisition of land, the construction of buildings, facilities, and other physical infrastructure, or the purchase of major equipment. Many of these funds receive and spend money obtained by borrowing. Indeed, most states finance some capital projects by borrowing rather than on a pay-as-you-go basis, and most use dedicated capital funds for at least some portion of their capital budget.

Many states have special funds for the finance, operation, and maintenance of large public enterprises like highways, bridges, other transportation projects, and utilities. These funds may derive revenues from particular taxes or fees whose receipts are earmarked for those funds, and they may borrow (and spend) money by pledging those earmarked funds. Many states have also created special trust funds, set apart from the rest of the state budget, to pay the pensions and health benefits of retired state and municipal employees or to serve as public guarantors for certain social welfare programs, such as workers' compensation insurance.

Thus, adding to the difficulty of ascertaining the scope of balanced budget strictures at the state level is that a significant portion of state fiscal activity takes place outside general funds, with the proportion varying considerably from state to state. In the 1990 fiscal year, state general funds nationwide accounted for 52.6 percent of state revenues and 54.4 percent of state expenditures, with general fund spending ranging from a low of 21 percent of total state spending in Wyoming to a high of 74 percent in Hawaii.[20] A more recent study found that in fiscal year 1993 only 48 percent of state spending came out of general funds. It is tempting to suggest that the distinction between general fund and non-general-fund spending is equivalent to the difference between expenditures for current services and capital expenses. But, as the Congressional Research Service has contended, it is implausible that in one state just one-fifth of the budget is for current expenses while in another three-quarters of expenditures are devoted to the same. Rather, these numbers imply that some current services are provided by some of the numerous special or capital funds. Given the ability of some special funds to incur debt, some current services are therefore probably financed by borrowing.[21]

At least some special and capital funds are not subject to constitutional balanced budget requirements, although this is usually difficult to determine from the constitutional texts. Balanced budget provisions "often do not specify a particular set of funds to which they apply."[22] The scope of the balanced budget stricture is, typically, not precisely determined by the constitution; rather, it often turns on the judgment of the very state officials that the constitutional provision is said to bind.

A 1985 GAO study reported that coverage by balanced budget language ran the gamut from as low as 46 percent to 100 percent of state spending, with the bulk of the states in the 47–66 percent range. Capital funds in twenty-five states and trust funds in twenty-two were found to be subject to balanced budget requirements.[23] A more recent (1992) NASBO study reported that in most states at least 75 percent of the budget is covered.[24] However, neither GAO nor NASBO distinguished between constitutional and statutory provisions, so it is uncertain how much of state spending is governed by constitutional balanced budget requirements.

Even when special funds or capital funds are subject to balanced budget requirements, investigators for the GAO found that the requirements were sometimes met by counting bond proceeds and other borrowings as revenues. In other words, in some cases capital funds may be deemed to be in balance when states do not spend more than they borrow, even if that means that they are spending more than their current tax and fee income.[25]

As a policy judgment and an accounting rule, it may be appropriate to exempt capital funds and trust funds from balanced budget requirements. However, as indicated, at least some capital and special funds are likely supporting operating expenditures as well as capital projects. Moreover, as will be seen in the next chapter, these funds may enable state governments to escape the discipline said to be imposed by balanced budget requirements. States may turn to capital funds and special funds to achieve nominal balance in the general fund, either by shifting operating expenses to these funds or by internal borrowing from funds that have current-year surpluses. If a special fund is intended for capital purposes and is authorized to incur debt, a transfer from that fund to the general fund may be a backdoor way for a state to cover its operating expenses with borrowed funds.

In short, the byzantine structure of state finances can undermine the discipline of balanced budget requirements that, on paper, seem quite severe. Although most states with balanced budget requirements do subject most of their funds to those requirements, there is considerable interstate variation, and in some states a substantial portion of state spending occurs outside of balanced budget requirements. When states do extend their balanced budget requirements to capital funds and other special funds they may deem those strictures satisfied by counting borrowed funds as current fiscal period receipts that may be used to offset current outlays. Thus, balanced budget requirements rarely if ever require that all current expenditures be paid for out of current revenues without borrowing.

Chapter 2

DO STATES ACTUALLY BALANCE THEIR BUDGETS?

The honest answer to the question of whether states achieve budgetary balance is that it is hard to tell. States write their own fiscal and accounting rules. According to NASBO, only seventeen states conform their budgets to generally accepted accounting principles (GAAP).[1] According to the GAO, "the differences between states' budgeting and accounting methods can produce markedly different results in reporting on their financial operations. States may report surpluses on a budgetary basis while at the same time reporting deficits on an accounting basis."[2] In other words, states may keep one set of books to meet the demands of creditors and the bond market and another to satisfy technical balanced budget requirements. This makes it hard to determine whether a state has actually balanced its budget in the popular sense, and it also makes it difficult to compare the fiscal track records of different states to assess whether constitutional balanced budget requirements make a difference. As the GAO noted, "there is variation among budgetary reporting given the degree of discretion states have in designing the budget structure and establishing reporting requirements to meet their own needs. Thus, the budgetary presentation for each state tends to be unique."[3]

Moreover, as discussed in the preceding chapter, some states are able to balance their budgets at year end by borrowing. Those states can satisfy the requirements of their state constitutions even though they run operating deficits. This is probably not what advocates of a balanced budget amendment envision.

SOME STATES WITH BALANCED BUDGET REQUIREMENTS RUN DEFICITS

Notwithstanding the regulatory leeway the states give themselves, some states—including states with constitutional balanced budget provisions—run deficits. Between the 1978 and the 1985 fiscal years, in twenty instances budget deficits were incurred in nine states—although five were in Vermont, the one state with neither a statutory nor a constitutional balanced budget requirement. More recently, between fiscal 1990 and fiscal 1993 ten states either ran a deficit that was carried into the next fiscal year or borrowed money to close the gap. States running deficits in this period included some of the nation's largest—California, New York, Pennsylvania, Illinois, Michigan—all of which have some constitutional balanced budget requirement.

California and New York have had particularly serious problems with deficits. For five out of seven years at the end of the 1980s and the start of the 1990s, California ran year-end deficits.[4] In the early 1990s, California budgets explicitly assumed the rollover of prior-year deficits. California ran a deficit of $1.9 billion at the end of fiscal 1990,[5] $3.3 billion at the end of fiscal 1991,[6] $2.8 billion at the end of fiscal 1993,[7] and $400 million at the end of fiscal 1994.[8] The state also ran deficits in 1982 and 1983.[9] Indeed, California has had considerable difficulties just getting a budget adopted, regardless of the prevailing economic conditions. Although its problems became acute only during the recession at the start of the 1990s, it missed its own constitutional deadline for adopting a budget in nineteen out of the twenty-two years before 1993.[10] The 1992 budget was adopted sixty-three days late.

New York has had a similarly checkered fiscal past. In the 1970s, the state ran deficits, relied on short-term notes to close out its fiscal years, and rolled one year's operating deficit over into the next. By 1983, New York had an accumulated operating deficit of $4 billion. The state ran operating deficits in six of the next eight years—that is, throughout the relatively prosperous 1980s—so that the accumulated deficit had swollen to $5.2 billion by fiscal 1990. In 1991, the state adopted a mechanism that effectively allowed it to bond a portion of the deficit. Nevertheless, the state ended fiscal 1991 more than $1.8 billion in the red, thereby pushing the accumulated deficit to an all-time high of $6.3 billion. This was cut to $2.6 billion by the end of fiscal 1993, attributable in significant part to the sale of $2.5 billion in bonds.[11] Like California, New York has had considerable difficulty in getting a budget adopted. In seventeen of the past twenty years, the state did not have a budget in place at the start of the fiscal year, with the delay lasting three months in 1994 and sixty-seven days in 1995.

Louisiana is another balanced budget state with a history of not balancing its budget. In the 1980s, the state racked up a $1.3 billion operating budget deficit, which it covered by internal borrowing from state accounts not subject to the balanced budget requirement and by deferring payments to vendors. Finally, in 1988 the state created the Louisiana Recovery District—a device to avoid the state constitution's restrictions on state debts—which was empowered to issue ten-year bonds to pay off the accumulated operating deficit.

Connecticut also recently resorted to borrowing to pay off an operating deficit. It ran operating deficits in 1989, 1990, and 1991. The 1989 deficit and part of the 1990 deficit were covered by withdrawals from the state's "rainy day fund," but, by the end of the 1990 fiscal year, the state had a cumulative operating deficit of $157 million. By the end of fiscal 1991 the cumulative deficit had ballooned to nearly one billion dollars. The state enacted an income tax and issued "economic recovery notes" to pay off the accumulated deficit, with interest, over five years. As a result, Connecticut's outstanding debt rose 33 percent from 1991 to 1994, and debt service exploded by 134 percent over a four-year period, while soaring from 6.7 percent to 12.8 percent of the state budget.[12]

Like Connecticut, Massachusetts ran back-to-back operating deficits at the start of the 1990s. Over a two-year period Massachusetts borrowed about $2 billion, including $1.4 billion in "deficit resolution bonds," to cover its deficits.[13] Between 1988 and 1994, Massachusetts's debt service rose 128 percent; interest expense went from representing 4.9 percent to 8.5 percent of the state budget.[14]

Other states that incurred substantial operating deficits at the start of the 1990s included Michigan[15] and Minnesota.[16] A complete listing of "balanced budget" states that have run deficits would be both tedious and beside the point. Even in hard times, most states do manage to achieve technical balance. But that balance is often quite technical indeed, accomplished by accounting gimmicks that include asset sales, deferral of payments, borrowing from trust funds, and drawing down reserve funds. A recent study of Michigan finances found that, despite the state constitution's balanced budget requirement, "the state has long made use of one-time revenues, funding delays and shifts, and creative accounting to get by each year. In almost every year since the late 1970s, these adjustments have been used to balance the budget."[17] During the 1980s, such fiscal sleights of hand accounted for about 10 percent of Michigan's general fund expenses. Only in 1991 did the state actually recognize a deficit on its books.

On an "honest" basis, do states balance their budgets? In other words, do they cover current expenditures with current revenues without interfund transfers, debt, or gimmicks? Many do but some do not. It appears that as many as half of the states may run deficits—although those deficits are typically modest, relative to the federal budget deficit, as a percentage of public spending. The Council of State Governments reported that in both 1991 and 1992 general expenditures outpaced general revenues in twenty-four states.[18] The council was careful to note that this did not mean the states were running deficits. Given the ability of the states to avoid generally accepted accounting principles in their budgetary systems, the council cautioned that "a difference between an individual government's total revenues and expenditures does not necessarily indicate a budget surplus or deficit."[19] Nevertheless, the council's figures are indicative of just how many states flirt with deficits despite their balanced budget requirements.

Similarly, the public finance specialists at the *State Budget & Tax News* found that at the end of fiscal 1994, twenty-seven states were in deficit functionally—in the sense that current expenditures exceeded current revenues—even though only one state, California, formally recognized a deficit at the end of fiscal 1994. Again, most of these deficits were quite modest, averaging less than 1 percent of state spending. These states covered the gap between revenues and expenditures and achieved nominal balance by drawing down reserve funds, borrowing from trust funds, and other accounting techniques.[20]

BALANCE BY TRICK: THE ROLE OF CREATIVE ACCOUNTING AND FISCAL GIMMICKRY

Over the years, the states have perfected a dazzling array of devices for achieving nominal budget balance. Some techniques are relatively simple.

Optimistic Forecasts

Faced with a looming $1.6 billion gap at the start of the 1995–96 fiscal year, New York, according to its state comptroller, cut the problem nearly in half by revising its estimates of likely spending downward and revenues under current programs upward.[21] Where a constitution merely requires the governor to submit, or the legislature to adopt, a balanced budget but does not limit short-term borrowing or carrying over an operating deficit into the next fiscal year, optimistic forecasts of economic conditions or expectations of federal grants can facilitate satisfaction of the state constitution's requirement.[22]

Rearranging the Budgetary Time Frame

More sophisticated gimmickry may involve manipulation of the fiscal period, accelerating revenues into the current period while deferring expenses until the next. This may involve treating revenues on an accrual basis—that is, counting them when they come due, even if they are not actually received by the state until the next fiscal period—while treating expenditures on a cash basis, counting them against the budget of the next period (if payment does not fall due until then) even if they are paid as a result of obligations incurred or services rendered in the current period. Although this may seem only to postpone the day of fiscal reckoning, if the state is able roll over its deficit, then, with the help of a little inflation, this stratagem can enable it to achieve nominal balance even with its ordinary expenses outpacing recurring revenues.

A classic instance of such accounting wizardry occurred in 1976, when Michigan changed its fiscal year from July 1–June 30 to October 1–September 30. That produced an initial fifteen-month fiscal year, in which the state picked up an additional three months' worth of revenue but because of the schedule for school aid payments incurred only one added education obligation. As a result, the state ended the fifteen-month year in surplus.[23] More commonly, states accelerate the payment of taxes due in a future fiscal period so that they can be counted as revenues in the present one.[24] New York uses these tricks so often that they have their own jargon: In New York budgetese they are known as "spin-ups."

Payment Deferrals

Similarly, to defer expenses from the current fiscal period into the future, states delay payments to employees, vendors, and local governments. Sometimes this is done formally, as when Michigan adopted cash accounting for Medicaid payments,[25] or when New York "rolled out" $145 million in school aid from one fiscal year into the next.[26] Massachusetts deferred until fiscal 1991 $1.26 billion in local assistance due in fiscal 1990.[27]

State attempts to postpone the payment of employee salaries have often been reversed by state courts, although the judicial action may not come until well after the end of the fiscal period. New York, for example, sought to cover a budget gap by utilizing a "lagged payroll" system in which state employees were paid for fifty weeks instead of fifty-two, with the remaining two weeks' salary to be paid to an employee only when he or she left the state system. Various versions of this plan were invalidated on constitutional grounds by both state and federal courts.[28] Similarly, the Florida supreme court struck down that state's postponement, and, ultimately, cancellation, of state employees' legally mandated pay increase.[29] The Massachusetts supreme judicial court invalidated a furlough program for state employees used to close out the 1991 fiscal year. The court's decision, however, was not reached until 1995.[30]

Pension Fund Reductions

Some states attempt to satisfy their balanced budget requirements by reducing contributions to public employee retirement trust funds. A common state practice is to recalculate upward the projected yields on trust fund investments in order to reduce the amount the state needs to pay into the fund to provide future retirees' benefits. In a more dramatic move, Michigan one year shifted its public school employees retirement system from an actuarial to a cash basis in order to limit its payment for retiree health benefits to the current year's costs rather than deposit in the fund the amount actuarially necessary to cover liabilities accrued during that year.[31]

Many of these efforts to defer payments to pension plans have also run into trouble in court. The Michigan supreme court held its state's shift to a cash basis to be unconstitutional, finding that "failing to fund pension benefits at the time they are earned amounts to borrowing against future budgets, or 'back door' spending."[32] The West Virginia supreme court condemned the legislature for "yield[ing] to the temptation of diverting pension funds in hard economic times" in order to use the revenues thus saved to cover budget shortfalls.[33] A court in California ruled that the diversion of "funds held in trusts for the exclusive benefit of the members and beneficiaries" of the public employees retirement system for budget balancing violated state employee rights.[34] Similarly, New York's highest court concluded that a legislative maneuver intended to balance the 1990 budget by reducing the state's contribution to the public employee retirement system was a "radical change" that "depletes several years of accrued retirement benefits involving millions of dollars and arguably destabilizes the fund."[35]

In general, states underfund their public employee pension plans. Underfunded pension liabilities do not show up in general fund budgets. In 1994, state pension funds had, on average, $88 in assets for every $100 in projected benefits.[36] This is the functional equivalent of shifting current year costs onto future generations—a central concern of proponents of a federal balanced budget amendment. As a justice of the Illinois supreme court observed in a 1994 case that challenged the underfunding of the state's public employee retirement systems, "the tax-paying citizenry of this State will bear the eventual burden of bailing out the systems from insolvency, an outcome made all the more predictable by such legislative maneuvering."[37]

Although many payment deferrals are predicated on formal legislative or administrative action—such as the refiguring of the anticipated yield on trust fund investments—some deferrals are more informal. Some states simply do not pay their bills when these come due. Illinois, for example, carried nearly one billion dollars in unpaid bills from fiscal year 1993 into fiscal year 1994.[38] Payments due to health care providers under the Medicaid program are especially likely candidates for deferral.[39]

Asset Sales, Refinancing, and Special Fund Transfers

Other accounting strategies involve realizing paper increases in income, or reductions in costs, that do not reflect real changes in the actual wealth or expenses of the state. High on the list of paper revenue gains are asset sales. New York, for example, included $50 million in future sales of assets to balance its 1995-96 budget, even though, as the state comptroller pointed out, the state had no list of properties to be sold, had engaged in no studies of whether willing and capable buyers existed, and had not considered whether other legal requirements—such as environmental impact statements or conditions attached to federal grants—constrained the state's ability to sell off any assets.[40] Massachusetts relied heavily on asset sales to balance its budgets in recent years. The fiscal 1992 budget called for $230 million in asset sales, although only $16 million was actually realized. The 1993 budget proposed $45 million in sales, and the 1994 budget another $51 million. Even if asset sales made under the pressure of balanced budget imperatives meet all expectations, and they generate proceeds that help close budget gaps, the long-term result may be fiscally wasteful. When a state sells an asset, such as a hospital or an office building, for less than its long-term value or for less than the cost of replacing the services the asset provides, then the sale is not only a financial gimmick but also leaves the state poorer than before.

Similarly, states may seek to reduce their current costs by refunding outstanding bonds. When debt is refinanced or reissued to take advantage of lower long-term interest rates, genuine savings are realized on behalf of the taxpayers. But if the cost of debt service is "reduced" simply by arranging to extend the time period during which debts are paid off, such reductions are achieved at the price of additional interest payments in the future. A critical evaluation of bond refundings in New York found that over a two-year period the state reaped a short-term savings of $200 million in debt service but added approximately $1 billion in eventual interest costs.[41]

Finally, states can take advantage of the arcane structure of state finances by using interfund transfers, whereby special funds that are not subject to balanced budget requirements lend or transfer money to the general fund. Moneys earmarked for capital projects or to guarantee social welfare programs can be used to cover an operating deficit. These interfund transfers undermine the purpose of creating a special, dedicated fund. Moreover, as many special funds are able to raise money by borrowing, interfund transfers have the effect of permitting a state to cover a portion of its operating costs with borrowed money.

New York's comptroller found that the state transferred $429 million from special funds to the general fund in order to balance the 1995–96 budget.[42] In the 1980s, California transferred tideland oil royalty funds, normally used for capital projects, to the general fund, and allocated interest earned in investment funds to the general fund.[43] Florida closed its fiscal 1991 budget gap through, among other actions, borrowing $151 million from trust funds without repayment.[44] Interfund transfers have on occasion been invalidated by state courts for diverting funds from their dedicated purposes.[45]

New York has developed a particularly ingenious technique known as "backdoor financing" that combines elements of the sale of assets with the manipulation of the interfund system. The state will sell a facility to a public authority, which is an entity created by the state and subject to its political direction but not treated as part of the state for budget purposes or for debt limitation provisions. The public authority will then lease the facility back to the state in return for rent payments that cover the cost of the sale plus any debt service the authority may owe if it issued bonds to raise the money to buy the state facility. Using this technique, New York sold the Attica Correctional Facility and a portion of interstate highway 287 to its Urban Development Corporation. The state obtained a onetime infusion of cash that enabled it to solve its immediate fiscal problem, but at the price of a long-term commitment to make lease payments. With the lease payments primarily covering debt service, this arrangement effectively permits the state to borrow to cover its operating costs. Not only do arrangements like the "sale" of Attica subvert balanced budget requirements, but also the byzantine structure of these deals typically places a greater financial burden on taxpayers than if the state had straight-forwardly borrowed the cash to cover an acknowledged deficit.

It is probably not possible to determine just how much states rely on accounting gimmicks and fiscal sleights of hand in balancing their budgets. The New York State comptroller reported that 3 percent of the state's 1995-96 general fund budget consisted of accounting tricks, and that the "short-sighted and extensive use of nonrecurring revenues" to cover operating costs had occurred regularly in the Empire State since 1989. In his view this "use of one-shots without adequate long-term planning merely defers difficult decisions and exacerbates the [state's] structural deficit."[46] A study of California's finances in the first four fiscal years of the 1990s calculated that the state had utilized $6.6 billion worth of "smoke and mirrors"—transfers from special funds, changes in accounting methods, and optimistic assumptions concerning economic growth, federal aid, and yield on state pension fund investments. That $6.6 billion closed about one-sixth of the total budget gap the state faced over the course of those four years.[47]

The GAO's survey of state finances at the start of the 1990s found that interfund transfers (including transfers from special contingency or "rainy day" funds), deferred payments, accounting changes, reductions in payments to pension plans, and short-term borrowing were responsible for about 19 percent of the gap-closing activity that occurred at the start of a fiscal period as part of the process of enacting a budget, and for reconciling about 36 percent of the budget gaps that emerged during a fiscal period. In the years the GAO studied, three states also failed to close midyear gaps and California enacted a budget that was unbalanced on its face.[48]

Of course, while relying on fiscal trickery, the states also make many hard choices. Most of the midyear fiscal shortfalls—60 percent in the early 1990s—were closed by spending cuts, just as most of the budget gaps at the start of the fiscal year were bridged either by spending cuts (49 percent) or revenue increases (32 percent). To repair the fiscal breaches that emerged during the recession in the early 1990s, 31 states enacted tax increases in 1990, 41 did likewise in 1991, and 40 increased taxes in 1992.[49] Some states, like New York, may be more prone to gimmickry than others. Most states appear to come reasonably close to paying for current expenditures out of current revenues most of the time, and some even run surpluses. When faced with unanticipated cost increases and unexpected revenue shortages most state governments make a serious effort to bring their general funds into balance. Many of the worst examples of fiscal manipulation occurred during recessions, as states struggled to deal with the fiscal consequences of an unexpected economic downturn without drastically altering their spending programs or their tax structures. This may make sense if the state's fiscal problems are really due to short-term economic phenomena and are not a reflection of a structural imbalance between expenditures and revenues.

The point of this review of state accounting gimmicks and fiscal sleights of hand is not to point a finger at the states. Rather, it is that the "fiscal discipline" of a constitutional balanced budget requirement does not preclude a certain reliance—considerable in some cases—on "smoke and mirrors" budgeting. Given the complex structure of state finances and the states' freedom to design their fiscal systems, it often may not be possible to determine whether a state has balanced its budget in the sense of paying for current-year expenditures with current-year revenues and without borrowing. That complexity also means that, constitutional requirements notwithstanding, "balance by trick" is a part of the fiscal practices of at least some of the states from time to time.

A balanced budget amendment would not necessarily produce a truly balanced budget, but might instead provide an impetus to unsound budgetary practices. The federal government is likely to be at least as clever as the states in deploying accounting techniques and other gimmicks that create balance in name only. Indeed, even in the absence of constitutional language, some of these gimmicks are already in place in the federal budgetary process. Federal legislation draws a distinction between "on-budget" and "off-budget" items for purposes of spending caps and deficit reduction targets.[50] The original Gramm-Rudman-Hollings Act excluded a long list of programs and activities from the definition of outlays used to measure the federal budget deficit and, consequently, exempted them from its deficit reduction procedure.[51] That list of exempt programs was extended in 1987.[52] As a leading expert on the federal budget noted, "there is no list of reasons as to why some program is not included in the budget totals; the decision is almost always political and can be changed depending on the year and the situation."[53]

Similarly, Congress has chartered more than forty[54] quasi-autonomous corporations—including such entities as the Financial Assistance Corporation (FICO), the Legal Services Corporation, the Federal Financing Bank, the Rural Telephone Bank, the Resolution Funding Corporation (REFCORP)—many of which have been given off-budget status.[55] Some of these federal government corporations, such as the Federal National Mortgage Association (Fannie Mae), the Student Loan Marketing Association (Sallie Mae), the Communications Satellite Corporation (Comsat), and the National Railroad Passenger Corporation (Amtrak), were created to enable the government to participate in commercial activity deemed in the public interest. But the increased political salience of the federal budget deficit in the 1980s and 1990s—and the enactment of legislation intended to control that deficit—appears to have led to the chartering of additional federal corporations in order to shelter government spending from the official calculation of the budget deficit. According to one recent study, FICO, REFCORP, and FAC, the Farm Credit System Financial Assistance Corporation (FICO and REFCORP were created as part of the savings and loan bailout while FAC was established to bail out the farm credit system),[56] "are really little more than accounting tricks designed to hide federal spending and debt."[57]

Both the states' extensive use of fiscal tricks to come into nominal compliance with their balanced budget requirements and the federal subterfuges used to evade the much less burdensome federal statutory deficit reduction rules demonstrate that formal requirements of budget discipline do not necessarily produce fiscal virtue.[58] Indeed, the evasive techniques prompted by legal requirements not only frustrate the intended restraint; they carry a price as well. Asset sales and deferrals of outlays that balance one year's budget often reduce income and increase costs in the long run. Moreover, the proliferation of accounting categories, special funds, and quasi-autonomous agencies—as well as the shifting of moneys among them—that are the hallmark of the circumventing balanced budget requirements obfuscates rather than clarifies fiscal conditions and reduces the ability of the citizenry to understand how their government works. Ironically, balanced budget requirements intended to increase popular control over government may actually result in making it more difficult for citizens to monitor their government and hold officials accountable for their actions.

MANIPULATING THE INTERGOVERNMENTAL SYSTEM

The states occupy a pivotal middle position in the intergovernmental system. A significant portion of state spending—a nationwide average of 28 percent in 1992—consists of aid to local governing bodies, such as cities, counties, and school districts.[59] By the same token, states receive a substantial share of their revenues—around 20 percent—in grants-in-aid from the federal government.[60] With so much of state budgeting intertwined with that of other governments, it is not surprising that manipulating the intergovernmental system has emerged as a critical aspect of state fiscal practices. In order to balance their budgets, states will seek to reduce their payments, or shift their costs, to local governments while obtaining further financial support from Washington. During the 1980s and early 1990s many states were quite successful in exploiting both strategies.

Shifting the burden of state deficits to local governments would appear to be less of a challenge. As a matter of law, local governments are creatures of their states and thus, for the most part, legally powerless either to compel the states to provide fiscal support or to prevent them from imposing costly obligations. Local assistance, a tempting target in many states, has been subject to cutbacks, deferral, or gubernatorial impoundment. As the Michigan supreme court found in affirming the governor's impoundment of revenue-sharing payments to local governments, "the State does have an obligation under the Constitution to balance the budget. It has no obligation to refrain from shifting the financial burdens of government to local government units."[61] Although some other state courts have invalidated unilateral gubernatorial impoundments of local assistance, local governments have little constitutional protection from legislatively authorized impoundments or other reductions in aid. Some state constitutions do entrench specified local assistance, such as support for schools.[62] But even when some aid to education is protected from midyear reductions, cutbacks in the unprotected portion of school aid may be used to balance the state budget.[63]

Deferrals, impoundments, or outright reductions in local assistance can play an important role in enabling states to balance their own budgets, albeit at the price of disrupting local finances. In the past decade or so, states have generally reduced the state contribution to local budgets. As a result, in every year since 1985 local taxes have risen faster than state taxes.[64] This process may accelerate during state fiscal crises. In Connecticut, aid to localities, including school districts, dropped from 38.4 percent of the state budget in 1991 to 34.4 percent in 1995.[65] In Massachusetts, over the period from 1988 to 1994, state support for localities, including local schools, dropped even more sharply, from 24.6 percent of the budget to 15.2 percent.[66] Between 1990 and 1994, California localities had to absorb $6.9 billion in aid cuts or new costs, accounting for a sixth of the funds used to close the state budget gap.[67]

State reductions in assistance to localities are not an accounting gimmick in the way that manipulations of the fiscal year or underfunding pension plans are since local aid cutbacks actually decrease the state's recurring costs. State law requires localities to provide certain services and regulates how they perform these functions. Local governments are, in many respects, arms of the state, carrying out traditional state programs in areas like education, public health, and social services. State reductions in local assistance do not shift costs onto future taxpayers, but they do shift the burden of joint state-local activities to local taxpayers. To that extent, the brunt of the "fiscal discipline" the balanced budget requirement is said to impose is borne not by the state governments subject to it but by local governments and local taxpayers (who are generally state taxpayers, too).

Looking to the other dimension of intergovernmental relations, states have proved adept at balancing their budgets with the assistance of federal funds, which played a vital role in enabling states in fiscal extremis in the early 1990s to close their budgetary gaps. In that period, federal aid to the states increased three times more rapidly than states' own tax revenues.[68] In California, federal funds spending increased by 47.8 percent between 1990 and 1993, even as state general fund spending declined slightly.[69] In Michigan, federal aid increased 38 percent between 1990 and 1993, going from 24.1 percent of state revenues to 28.8 percent.[70] In Connecticut, federal aid rose even more dramatically, from 11 percent of state revenues in 1987 to 20 percent in 1995.[71]

The driving force behind the increase in federal aid has been Medicaid, and especially the states' clever exploitation of the terms of federal assistance for the program. Medicaid provides federal funds to match qualified state expenditures on health care, primarily care for the indigent and long-term nursing care for the elderly. The federal contribution in a state depends on a formula that factors in the per capita income of the state. The federal government pays at least 50 percent of Medicaid costs in each state, ranging up to 83 percent in the poorest state and averaging around 57 percent nationwide.[72]

In the late 1980s, the states moved adroitly to shift more of their traditional public health costs to Medicaid by having these costs qualify for federal Medicaid reimbursement whenever Medicaid-eligible people are served, and by obtaining additional funds for care provided in poor areas. More important, the states invented the so-called bootstrap financing technique, by which hospitals and other health care providers were persuaded either to make voluntary donations to state Medicaid-funded programs or to consent to state taxation, with the resulting revenues earmarked for Medicaid programs. These donations and tax dollars from providers then became eligible for federal Medicaid matching money. Ultimately, the donations and provider tax payments were returned to their original sources, but first the states netted the federal matching funds they precipitated. In effect, the providers were held harmless, but their "donations" and "taxes" were used to leverage an expanded federal contribution to state health programs.

Once the bootstrap technique was perfected at the end of the 1980s, its use spread rapidly. In the 1990 fiscal year, just 5.8 percent of state Medicaid spending came from sources, such as donations and provider taxes, outside of state general funds. By 1992, when the federal government began to crack down on the practice, 19.3 percent of state Medicaid spending came from these sources. In 1993, the figure reached 21.1 percent. Exploiting this loophole in federal law, state Medicaid spending rose 26.9 percent in 1991 and 27.9 percent in 1992, with three-eighths of the increase attributable to provider taxes and donations.[73] In some states Medicaid spending exploded, rising 61 percent in Louisiana from 1991 to 1992, 60 percent in Missouri, 90 percent in West Virginia, and 105 percent in New Hampshire.[74] In Louisiana, where Medicaid spending benefited from a 72 percent federal match, Medicaid amounted to 26.5 percent of the 1993 state budget.[75]

Although Medicaid bootstrap financing may be an extreme case of states' balancing their budgets with federal assistance, it is not unprecedented. A study of the state and local response to recession in the early 1980s found that subnational governments were skilled at using federal grants to pick up the costs of employment, urban development, social services, and health programs these governments had traditionally provided out of their own funds.[76]

State exploitation of the terms of federal aid is not technically an accounting gimmick since the increase in funds in one year does not entail a price to be paid later. But, like the resort to accounting tricks, the manipulation of the intergovernmental system indicates states have found ways of living with constitutional "fiscal discipline" that do not involve either tightening their own belts or internalizing through taxation the costs of their programs.

The implications for a federal balanced budget constitutional amendment are a little uncertain. As it sits atop the governmental pyramid, the federal government is not in a position to obtain assistance from elsewhere. On the other hand, a federal government compelled to balance its budget would surely follow the lead of the states and resort to reductions in assistance to other tiers of government as a preeminent fiscal strategy.

Indeed, the real impact of a federal balanced budget amendment could be on the states' ability to balance their own budgets. Not only would new federal aid be unavailable to close budgetary gaps during times of fiscal stress, but the level of ongoing federal support for states and localities would probably be reduced, thereby creating new strains on the states and new hurdles for them to overcome.

Chapter 3

THE SEPARATION OF POWERS

Although the balanced budget amendment debate has focused on the role of constitutional requirements in preventing deficits, balanced budget provisions may have important consequences for the distribution of power among the different branches of government. State balanced budget provisions, along with other state constitutional directives affecting public finances, have tended to strengthen the executive branch relative to the state legislature. Moreover, by turning a fiscal standard into a rule of law, they have implicated the judiciary in budgetary matters traditionally left to the legislative and executive branches.

EMPOWERING THE EXECUTIVE

Balanced budget requirements are part of a legal framework that, in most states, shifts the balance of power away from the legislature and toward the governor. The governor can play an influential role in three stages of the budget process: initial submission, enactment, and implementation. State constitutions, legislation, case law, and administrative practices tend to expand the power of the governor at all three stages.

In many states the governor takes the lead in framing the budget debate. In several states—including California, New York, Michigan, and Massachusetts—the principal constitutional requirement is that the governor submit a balanced budget plan to the legislature. In these states, the governor sets the terms of legislative deliberation over the budget, with his spending and revenue priorities dominating the process. Whether as a matter of constitutional text, statutory prescription, or political practice, most states utilize such an executive budget system.

Moreover, the constitutions of forty-three states vest in their governors line-item veto authority, so that the governor may veto individual spending items without having to veto the entire budget. In ten states, owing either to constitutional text or judicial interpretation, the governor has the power to reduce a budget item. Line-item veto authority, and even more so the authority to force spending cuts, greatly enhances the power of the governor vis-a-vis the legislature in the enactment of a budget.

But the greatest departure from the balance of executive and legislative power at the federal level is at the implementation stage. Many states grant their governors unusually broad powers to reduce spending after a budget has been enacted without having to return to the legislature for approval. Thus, the Missouri constitution provides: "The governor may control the rate at which any appropriation is expended during the period of appropriation by allotment or other means, and may reduce the expenditures of the state or any of its agencies below their appropriations whenever the actual revenues are less than the revenue estimates upon which the appropriations were based."[1] The Missouri supreme court has held that this "broadly authorizes the Governor to balance the state's budget in the event that state revenues fall below the revenue expectations."[2] The North Carolina constitution is even more emphatic, declaring that "to insure that the State does not incur a deficit for any fiscal period, the Governor *shall* continually survey the collection of the revenue and shall effect the necessary economies in State expenditures . . . whenever he determines that receipts during the fiscal period . . . will not be sufficient to meet budgeted expenditures."[3]

According to the Council of State Governments, some forty-two states, either by constitutional provision or by statute, allow their governors to make cuts in budgeted spending without legislative authorization.[4] To be sure, the governor's power to cut may be subject to limits or restrictions. The governor may be constrained to make only across-the-board percentage reductions, rather than reductions targeted on specific programs. Some states set a ceiling on the size of the governor's cuts. The governor of Connecticut may cut up to 5 percent of an appropriation; the governor of Louisiana may cut an appropriation by 10 percent; the governor of Maryland is permitted to slash most executive branch appropriations by 25 percent.[5] Some states limit the governor's power of spending reduction to executive branch agencies or state operations while protecting other functions, such as education or local aid. Finally, some states require the governor to consult with, or obtain the consent of, other officials. (In Florida, for example, the governor and cabinet—which consists of independently elected executive branch officers—together "may establish all necessary reductions in the state budget."[6] Similarly, the Michigan supreme court recently held that the governor could undertake certain interfund transfers to balance the state's budget with the consent of the State Administrative Board, consisting of the governor and five other executive branch officials, including one appointed by the governor.)[7] Even with these restrictions, state governors enjoy considerable authority to reshape state budgets over the course of the fiscal period following legislative enactment.

Governors have responded to revenue shortfalls by freezing hiring, promotions, equipment purchases, and contracting; imposing furloughs; temporarily shutting down the state government; and impounding appropriated funds. Although typically the governor's power to respond to fiscal crises is limited to reducing spending, the governor of Minnesota is authorized to suspend tax indexing[8] and thereby increase revenues.[9]

Some governors have argued that an implied power of impoundment is inherent in a constitutional balanced budget requirement. This claim has received a mixed reception in state courts. Citing the "mandate to balance the State's budget," the Rhode Island supreme court upheld the governor's executive order shutting down the state government for ten business days in order to balance the 1990–91 budget.[10] The state's highest court, however, in a close decision concluded that the governor could not impound local assistance.[11]

The New York court of appeals reached a similar resolution of the impoundment question. Noting that the state constitution requires merely that the governor propose a balanced budget and does not require actual balance at the end of the fiscal year, the court held that the balanced budget provision could not be the source of authority to impound local aid.[12] New York, however, permits gubernatorial impoundment of appropriations for state agencies.

The Massachusetts supreme judicial court split the issue a little differently, holding that the governor may not impound appropriated funds "on the basis of his views regarding the social utility or wisdom of the law," but that the chief executive does have the "discretion to exercise his judgment not to spend money in a wasteful fashion" where a reduction would be necessary for balanced budget purposes. The Massachusetts court relied on the state's balanced budget requirement to support its determination that proposed legislation completely banning impoundments would be unconstitutional.[13]

Governors have done better in relying on balanced budget strictures to defend impoundments authorized by legislation when the relevant law has been challenged as a violation of the constitutional ban on the delegation of legislative power to the executive branch. Courts in Louisiana and Ohio sustained the delegation of broad budget-cutting authority to the governor.[14] The Alaska supreme court invalidated a broad delegation of power to withhold appropriated spending[15] but subsequently upheld a narrower statute.[16] A divided Florida supreme court struck down the legislature's delegation of power to the governor to alter the budget in the event of a revenue shortfall, over the objections raised in a sharp dissent that contended that under the state's balanced budget amendment "the governor has a constitutional obligation to preclude the expenditure of funds in excess of revenue."[17] Subsequently the Florida constitution was amended to give the governor, in consultation with the cabinet, authority to reduce spending during the fiscal year.

In short, governors have far more power relative to their legislatures with respect to fiscal matters than the president enjoys vis-à-vis Congress. The general shift of budgetary discretion to the executive at the state level makes it difficult to isolate and evaluate the significance of the balanced budget requirement itself in leading states to fiscal equilibrium. Balanced budget provisions work in tandem with other elements of state government, such as the executive budget system, the line-item veto, and enhanced gubernatorial authority to reduce spending during the fiscal year. Balanced budget requirements may be more likely to achieve their aims if the executive can threaten to veto or reduce budget items or can take unilateral steps during the fiscal year to impound appropriations.

Federal balanced budget politics may well lead to an increase in presidential power over fiscal matters. Presidents Reagan and Bush always combined their call for a balanced budget amendment with a call for a presidential line-item veto, claiming that both were necessary to put Washington's fiscal house in order.[18] In 1996, Congress passed and President Clinton signed into law a statute giving the president a form of line-item veto authority, effective in 1997. This statute, however, does not resolve the debate over the scope of the veto power since it is uncertain whether a statutory line-item veto is constitutional. Moreover, Congress could attempt to limit the effect of the statutory line-item veto by excluding particular budget measures or items from the statute's reach. A balanced budget amendment could provide support for a more authoritative and binding line-item veto constitutional amendment, as well as for other measures, such as a grant of impoundment authority, that would enhance the president's fiscal powers.

More subtly, the president could make a case that the balanced budget amendment gives him a tacit line-item veto or impoundment authority, as many governors have similarly claimed to find. Although this argument has gotten a mixed reception in state courts, it is impossible to tell how it would fare in federal court. But the possibility that the balanced budget amendment would prove to be a source of implied presidential power over spending in the event of a revenue shortfall or a sudden economic downturn cannot be dismissed.

Enhanced presidential control of the budget is likely to lead to power over other matters. The debate over the balanced budget amendment must consider not simply the wisdom of mandating fiscal practices but the potential consequences for a change in executive-legislative relations.

THE ROLE OF THE COURTS

In arguing that a balanced budget amendment will discipline the political branches, proponents implicitly rely on judicial enforcement of the amendment's obligations. A constitutional article by itself is merely a declaration of principles, no more binding than the paper on which it is printed unless it is enforced, and in our system the courts play a leading role in spelling out constitutional principles and compelling the other branches of government to abide by them. Yet many people—including proponents of the balanced budget amendment—are uncomfortable with courts' tackling technical fiscal questions, such as the accuracy of economic forecasts or the appropriateness of accounting classifications, or entering the heated political debate over what actions to take in the event elected officials fail to balance the budget. Thus, although court enforcement may be necessary to make a constitutional command effective in constraining the legislature and the executive, balanced budget amendment proponents seek to discount concerns that judges might make fiscal policy, order spending priorities, or pass on the sufficiency of revenues.

Surprisingly, there has been relatively little balanced budget litigation in the state courts, and most of that has been addressed to ancillary matters rather than the central question of whether a state has actually adopted a balanced budget. Overall, state judges have played very little role in elaborating or enforcing state balanced budget requirements.

State courts have been called upon to hear challenges to some of the techniques states have used to balance their budgets: employee wage freezes, deferrals, and furloughs; failures to make payments to pension funds; diversions of pension fund and other trust fund moneys to the general fund; reductions in local government assistance. As already noted, balanced budget provisions have played a role in cases involving the scope of the governor's line-item veto power or impoundment authority, or the constitutionality of the legislature's delegation of broad authority to the governor to cut funds or rejuggle spending priorities during the fiscal year. In all of these cases, the balanced budget language has been cited as a justification for a cutback, nonpayment, or transfer of funds. In other words, the balanced budget requirement has been a *shield*, used by a governor or state to defend against the claim that a belt-tightening action violates some legal right of persons affected by it. Its success as a defensive weapon has been mixed, particularly in cases involving state failures to abide by contracts with employees or raids on pension and insurance funds.

But constitutional mandates have only rarely been deployed as a *sword* to compel a state to balance its budget or even to force a state to defend its assertion that its budget is balanced. Indeed, there does not appear to be any case in the last several decades in which a state court actually invalidated a state budget for failure to satisfy a constitutional balance requirement or compelled a state to take action to bring its budget into balance.

The question of whether a state's budget actually complies with its own constitutional requirements has, apparently, been litigated just twice in recent decades—both times about twenty years ago. In *Bishop v. Governor of Maryland*,[19] taxpayers challenged Maryland's 1976–77 budget, claiming that it was balanced only because it relied on two optimistic contingencies: revenues from state-lottery-related statutes not yet enacted at the time the budget was signed into law and the prospect of an extension of the federal revenue sharing program, which was set to expire. The Maryland constitution defined a balanced budget as one in which "estimated revenues [are] available to pay the appropriations." Plaintiffs contended that, as the budget counted on revenues not "available" when it was enacted, it was unbalanced.

The trial court held that "estimated revenues" could include contingent revenues and thus found the constitutional requirement satisfied. The Maryland appellate court did not rule on the appeal until nearly six months after the end of the fiscal year, by which time both the federal and state contingencies had come to pass and the estimated revenues had been collected. One appellate judge, asserting that "there have been a number of instances within the last 20 or 25 years in which Governors of Maryland in order to achieve a balanced budget have resorted to some ingenious bookkeeping measures such as a shift in the calculated time for receipt of certain revenues," urged the court to consider whether, under the constitution, contingent revenues could be counted in balancing the state budget. But the court dismissed the case as moot.

The other case in which plaintiffs vainly sought to enforce a state constitution's balanced budget strictures is *Wein v. Carey*,[20] which involved a challenge to New York's issuing of short-term tax and revenue anticipation notes to balance its budget. The New York constitution bars the issuance of state debt without a referendum. However, "debts in anticipation of the receipt of taxes or revenues" are exempt from the referendum requirement, provided these debts are repaid within one year of the date of issue.[21] The exemption for short-term notes enables the state to "cover unanticipated budgetary deficiencies."[22] By the time of *Wein v. Carey*, however, two successive annual deficits had occurred; short-term notes had been issued in both years. There was a plan to issue still more anticipatory notes in 1977–78, which plaintiffs argued "would be an ill-disguised 'rollover' or unconstitutional refinancing of a planned deficit."[23]

Despite the multiyear deficits and the state's repeated reliance on short-term notes, a unanimous court of appeals—New York's highest court—dismissed the case with an opinion that seems intended to make it most difficult for plaintiffs ever to litigate successfully a balanced budget claim in New York. The court stressed there was no constitutional authority "to permit judicial review of a State budget plan directly."[24] The court would consider only whether the issuing of notes was unconstitutional, not the budget itself.

The plaintiff bore the burden of proving not merely that the state would be unable to pay off the notes within one year of issue without additional borrowing but also that the state's claim that it could do so was "dishonest." This focus on truthful intent rather than on the accuracy of the state's forecasting created a "formidable" hurdle for plaintiffs. Ultimately, the court determined that the deficits and rollover of short-term notes in the years immediately prior—years in which the state had maintained that the budget was balanced when enacted—gave no support to plaintiff's allegation that the state's claim to be able to repay the latest debt without a further rollover was dishonest:

> The fact is that there may be an indefinite series of deficits honestly suffered. All that is necessary to produce the result are successive years of unpredictable shortfalls in revenues or rises in required spending beyond estimates. Depressed economic conditions can affect both sides of the balance. Catastrophes, emergencies, or, in smaller scale, significant needs may arise, which, if unanticipated, may upset the balance on one side or the other.[25]

Nor would the court itself consider the veracity of the state's revenue and expenditure estimates: "Assuming it were feasible to convert a courtroom into a superauditing office to receive and criticize the budget estimates of a State with an $11 billion budget, the idea is not only a practical monstrosity but would duplicate exactly what the Legislature and Governor do together, in harmony or in conflict, most often in conflict, for several months of each year."[26]

The court indicated that there might be some situations in which the state's budget numbers were unreasonable on their face, such as if they projected a "tripling of the estimates of personal income tax revenue, without a change in the tax rate, in a period in which the economy appears to be in a plateau or in decline" or failed to include constitutionally mandated costs in the estimate of expenditures.[27] Apart from these extreme cases, the court would be obliged to accept the state government's fiscal judgment. As a result, although the New York court reads its state constitution to preclude the intentional rollover of the state's deficit, the court has held itself bound to accept the state's assertion that the budget is balanced—and barred from examining the fiscal facts that might support or undermine that assertion—even if past practice raises serious questions about the accuracy of the state's claim.

Bishop and *Wein* are indicative of state courts' reluctance to evaluate state budget estimates and determine whether they have achieved balance. And these are cases state courts actually heard and decided. The vast majority of instances of questionable budget balancing do not result in judicial oversight at all. Three reasons may be offered as to why this is so.[28] First, there is the question of standing. The *Wein* case got as far as it did because of New York's liberal standing rule, which gives citizens and taxpayers broad authority to challenge allegedly unconstitutional actions in court. By contrast, many jurisdictions require that a plaintiff allege a government's action is the cause of some discrete personal injury before the court will hear the plaintiff's claim. The failure to balance a budget may violate the constitution, but few can demonstrate that they have a "personal stake" in a balanced budget. It is hard to argue that one is personally injured by the state's failure to raise taxes or by the size of its expenditure program. On the contrary, budget-balancing actions—not deficits—are more likely to result in harm to individuals, as the suits by employees, pension plan beneficiaries, and local governments aggrieved by state cutbacks demonstrate.

Second, the New York court's revulsion at the "practical monstrosity" of evaluating the state's budget is indicative of a general judicial reluctance to pass judgment on economic forecasts, revenue and expenditure projections, and accounting techniques. Courts may be concerned about their lack of expertise in this area, or about the dangers of involving themselves in the political struggles that often surround these decisions. The Supreme Court has announced that, under the "political question" doctrine, federal courts ought to avoid cases that would entangle the courts in partisan controversy. Although the Court has often put the doctrine to one side and taken on questions that could be labeled political, it may be taken more seriously by state courts.[29]

Third, there is the problem of remedies. What is a court to do if it finds a budget out of balance? Raise taxes? Which taxes and how much? Cut spending? Again, which programs and how much? This is the real "political question" shadowing a case involving budgets. Balancing a budget entails the resolution of conflicting expenditure and revenue priorities and a determination of the proper size and role of government in the economy and society. These questions are at the heart of politics and well beyond the special province of the courts. State constitutions rarely provide for remedies in the event that a state fails to balance its budget.

Although courts have done little to compel states to abide by balanced budget requirements, they are nevertheless players in state fiscal decisionmaking. Court decisions shape the nature of the gubernatorial line-item veto, define impoundment authority, and constrain the ability of states to raid pension and trust funds, furlough state employees, or block scheduled pay increases.[30] Unlike the federal Constitution, state constitutions give considerable attention to fiscal matters. Many state constitutions limit expenditures or revenues, restrict debt, or require states to set aside a portion of revenues in so-called rainy day funds. State courts have treated these provisions as presenting justiciable questions of constitutional law, and have asserted their independent authority to consider and define key fiscal concepts—like "debt," "revenue," "appropriation"—when they appear in a state's constitution.

In a 1994 decision, for example, the Alaska supreme court underscored the political consequences of constitutional fiscal mandates. Alaska's constitution requires the state to maintain a "budget reserve fund," from which the state may withdraw money in the event "the amount available for appropriation" in one year is less than the amount appropriated in the prior year, subject to certain restrictions. When the state legislature enacted a law giving a narrow reading to "amount available for appropriation," the court invalidated the statute. It rejected the argument that because appropriations are ordinarily the domain of the legislature, it should defer to the legislature's definition of "amount available for appropriation," declaring, "The proper interpretation of a constitutional provision is a question of law to which this court applies its independent judgment."[31] The legislature's role in appropriations would have had no effect on the court's authority to define terms used in the constitution.

Similarly, the Florida supreme court recently asserted its authority to define the word "revenue" in the context of that state's newly enacted constitutional amendment limiting the growth of state revenues.[32]

In short, the state judicial experience with balanced budget and other fiscal provisions of state constitutions has two implications for a federal balanced budget amendment. First, the paucity of state cases construing and enforcing balanced budget requirements raises a serious question about the importance of such provisions in compelling states to balance their budgets. Amendment proponents contend that a constitutional mandate is necessary to discipline the executive and the legislature. This assumes it will actually be enforced against elected officials who otherwise would plunge the budget into deficit. The absence of judicial decisions may be the "dog that didn't bark"—that is, the evidence indicates that balanced budget strictures are not actually being enforced against governors and legislatures. That does not mean that states are failing to balance their budgets. Rather, it suggests that constitutions are not doing the work of forcing state budgets into balance.

Second, the presence of fiscal language in a constitution opens the door to judicial involvement in budgetary policymaking and politics. Fiscal constitutional provisions transform public finance into constitutional law. State courts have significantly influenced many aspects of state finances, especially, as will be seen in the next chapter, state debt. Although balanced budget amendments have not, thus far, been a major focus of state litigation, federal courts could prove to be less reticent in using a constitutional amendment to assert a role in federal fiscal decisionmaking.

Chapter 4

THE LESSONS OF
RESTRICTIONS ON DEBT

M ost state constitutions restrict the freedom to borrow. Indeed, many balanced budget amendment proponents rely on debt limits in tabulating which states have balanced budget language written into their constitutions. The restrictions on debt are therefore directly relevant to an appraisal of the state balanced budget experience. The history of state debt limits, however, suggests that these provisions have done more to affect the type of debt states issue, raise borrowing costs, fragment state governments, and empower state courts than to preclude states from incurring debt.

State constitutions include a variety of debt limitations. Some bar state debt outright.[1] Others impose low dollar limits on the amount of debt a state can incur.[2] A few states set the amount of debt or debt service as a fraction of the state's taxable wealth or of state revenues.[3] Most commonly, states rely on a procedural restriction: debt may not be incurred without the approval of a majority of state voters in a referendum,[4] or a supermajority vote in the legislature, or both.[5]

In practice, even in states with absolute bans or very low dollar limits on the amount of debt, the real constraint is procedural. State constitutions may be amended—and proscriptions against borrowing thereby circumvented—to authorize specific bond issues. Typically, the legal requirements for a constitutional amendment—legislative supermajority, voter approval—are no more onerous than the hurdles a bond issue must overcome in states that rely solely on procedural restrictions. Thus, a constitution that prohibits debt in general may be amended to authorize borrowings for particular purposes. The Alabama constitution, for example, bars debt but contains thirty-three amendments authorizing specific bond issues.[6] More important, constitutional limits have been significantly eroded by the skill of state governments and their lawyers in persuading courts that a range of borrowing techniques are not "debt" in accordance with the meaning given by state constitutions.

State evasion of constitutional debt limits began with the so-called *special fund doctrine* in the late nineteenth century. That doctrine focused on borrowing to finance the construction of physical infrastructure—projects that, once in operation, could generate revenue sufficient to pay off the debt incurred. To build a bridge, the state would borrow money, promise to impose a toll on users of the facility, and pledge the proceeds for repayment of the loans. State courts quickly agreed that so long as the state limited its obligation to the "special fund" of moneys generated by the project and disclaimed any duty to come up with additional funds should the revenue attributable to the project fall short, these bonds were not "debt" within the meaning of state constitutional restrictions.

Once established, the special fund concept quickly spread well beyond the financing of projects that would generate revenue for the repayment of the debt. In theory, these projects did not cost state taxpayers any money but rather paid for themselves out of user charges. States proposed, and state courts frequently agreed, that a borrowing ought not to be treated as "debt" if the medium for repayment were limited to some specified sources of revenues—not just revenues generated by the project financed—and the state disclaimed a general repayment obligation if the specified revenue sources proved inadequate. These projects could cost the state money. Repaying the debt would involve a long-term commitment of funds—funds necessarily diverted from other state spending purposes or from tax relief. But because the state's obligation was limited and did not involve a commitment of its "full faith and credit," legislatures and their lawyers were often able to persuade state courts to refrain from characterizing such an undertaking as "debt." In effect, the special fund idea evolved into a rule of limited obligation: if the state limits its obligation, then even if there is a long-term commitment of its funds, this is not considered "debt."

Over time, the states developed two types of debt. "General obligation" bonds—also known as "full faith and credit" debt—involve the state's pledge of its general revenue-raising capacity rather than any specific revenue source. This is "debt" within the meaning of state constitutions. By contrast, "revenue bonds"—that is, bonds repaid out of specified revenues—or "nonguaranteed debt," so called because the state does not guarantee the use of any revenues other than those specified toward repayment, are often exempt from constitutional regulation. The history of debt restrictions has been a chronicle of state fiscal ingenuity in developing new instruments for borrowing while persuading courts that these instruments do not create debt in the constitutional sense.

Two particularly striking instances of such state legal legerdemain are lease-payment agreements and moral obligation bonds. Lease-payment agreements are used to finance debt for the construction of state facilities. The idea is that some entity other than the state—a private party or a quasi-governmental agency not subject to the debt restriction—borrows the money needed. The state agrees to a long-term lease of the facility, promises to pay rent, and authorizes the borrower to pledge the state's rent as security for repayment of the money borrowed to finance construction. In many states, so long as the legislation authorizing long-term lease makes the state's duty to pay rent subject to annual appropriation or annual termination, rather than an ironclad obligation, courts do not treat lease-payment financing as state "debt."[7] As the New Jersey supreme court observed in upholding such an arrangement, state courts have exhibited an "approach . . . of broad tolerance to permit public financing devices of needed facilities not constituting on their face present, interest-bearing obligations of the State itself."[8]

The key to evading the constitutional debt restriction is avoidance of an absolute commitment to repay a debt out of state revenues. If, however, the state is relying on a new, untested, or potentially unreliable revenue source, it may need to give lenders some additional security. Yet, in order to avoid the constitutional debt prohibition, such security must not actually bind the state to pay debt service out of general funds. One especially creative technique of binding the state in the eyes of lenders but not of state courts is the moral obligation bond. The state may pledge its moral obligation to bondholders to appropriate what is needed for current payments out of general revenues if the special revenues pledged as debt service fall short. Such a moral obligation is not legally binding; the payment of any debt service is within the discretion of the legislature. As such, moral obligation bonds are not "debt" in the meaning of state constitutions. Yet, as a practical political matter, moral obligation bonds, like lease financing, have proved quite binding. Few states have been willing to risk their credit ratings and incur additional interest charges for other debts by not living up to their moral obligations.

As a result of revenue bonds, lease-payment arrangements, moral obligation bonds, and voter approval of general obligation debt, the states have incurred a great deal of debt, and state borrowing has grown rapidly in the past three decades. Total state debt was $21.6 billion in 1962 and $372 billion at the end of fiscal 1992. Between 1986 and 1992, year-to-year increases in total state debt ranged between 6.8 and 8.6 percent.[9] Combined state debts as a percentage of gross domestic product rose from 1.5 percent in 1949 to 4.2 percent in 1970 to 6.2 percent in 1992.[10] At the end of fiscal 1992, state debt outstanding per capita was $1,461. Even states with absolute constitutional prohibitions on debt still had some outstanding debt.[11]

The principal impact of the debt restrictions appears to be on the form, not the amount, of state debt: Most state debt today is nonguaranteed—73 percent, up from 14 percent in 1942 and 50 percent in 1962. Nine states have no long-term general obligation debt, but all states have some nonguaranteed debt.[12] Although some state courts define "debt" broadly to require some revenue bonds and lease-payment financing to obtain voter approval, and some states have amended their constitutions to impose some constraints on nonguaranteed debt, in many states nonguaranteed debt is still not "debt" strictly by the state constitution.[13] As needs for borrowed funds have grown, many states have evaded debt proscriptions by shifting to nonguaranteed debt.

The rise of nonguaranteed debt to evade state constitutional debt restrictions has had several consequences. First, it increases the costs of borrowing. Nonguaranteed debt is by definition less secure than debt that carries a pledge of the full faith and credit of the state.

As a result, interest rates on nonguaranteed debt are higher than on general obligation bonds. Moreover, nonguaranteed debt is usually more complicated in form than full-faith-and-credit debt. The issuer has to make pledges to lenders concerning the operation of the facility financed by the borrowing, the depositing of revenues in funds dedicated to debt service, reserve funds, carrying charges during the period of construction, and so on. Nonguaranteed bonds therefore carry higher legal, administrative, underwriting, and insurance costs. As one treatise on state finance noted, "the very complexity of these instruments has increased issuance costs dramatically."[14]

Second, constitutional debt restrictions have contributed to the fragmentation of state government. To persuade state courts that various debt instruments backed by special funds did not commit the full faith and credit of the state, many states chose to spin off the entities issuing the debt into separate, quasi-autonomous bodies. In effect, the special funds were housed in agencies that were made relatively independent of the state government. These agencies—variously known as public authorities, public benefit corporations, commissions, or special districts—are now a central feature of state governance, with control over many state facilities, particularly in areas like transportation and economic development. Even in states that treat some revenue bonds or lease-payment financing as debt, public authority debt is generally not subject to constitutional limits.

The heads of public authorities are generally appointed by governors or other state officials, but once in office they are protected from removal and may serve terms that run longer than those of the people who appoint them. As a result, they are typically less accountable to and less subject to control by elected officials and the public. The placing of many state facilities in the hands of quasi-autonomous bodies not directly responsible to the governor and legislature may interfere with the coordination of functions and the efficient provision of state services.

There is a direct connection between debt restrictions and the proliferation of public authorities. States with constitutional debt limits have more authorities than those without them. In the states, on average, 25 percent of public infrastructure debt is issued by public authorities, but in states with constitutional bounds on debt, the figure is 34 percent. In states where the debt limit applies to revenue bonds, 46 percent of infrastructure debt is issued by public authorities.[15]

The connection between state debt limits and the rise of public authorities is seen most plainly in public building authorities—entities created by the states to finance the construction of public facilities. They issue the debt, build the structures, and pay debt service to lenders from the lease payments made to them by the state agencies that use the facilities. They exist to circumvent debt limits since their only revenues are rent income from state treasuries and their only purpose is to finance and construct facilities for state use. Fifty percent of all states with debt limits have public building authorities—and that rises to 92 percent of the states whose constitutional debt limits apply to revenue bonds.[16]

Third, as a result of the proliferation of public authorities, debt limits may actually undermine rather than reinforce balanced budget requirements. Although authorities are legally independent of the state, an authority and a state government may develop a politically cozy relationship. The state can then borrow from the public authority to obtain funds necessary to cover a deficit, and neither the loan from the authority nor the debt incurred by the authority to lend the money to the state will be treated as debt within the premises of the state constitution. Alternatively, a state may be able to create a public authority, authorize it to borrow money, provide it with a revenue stream to pay off its debts, and direct the authority to use the proceeds of its borrowing to help out the state. This balances the budget with borrowed funds but avoids any of the restrictions on state debt.

A classic instance of a state's manipulation of an existing authority was a device New York used in 1990 to obtain $230 million vital to balancing its budget. The state authorized the sale and leaseback of two state-owned assets, the Attica Correctional Facility and interstate highway 287, to an autonomous, state-created entity, the Urban Development Corporation (UDC). The sales were financed by UDC bonds, which in turn were secured by the pledge of "rents" paid by the state to lease back Attica and the highway. UDC did not seek voter approval for its bond issue, and the state did not seek voter approval for its leaseback commitment. The authority device provided a handy way for the state to incur long-term debt to balance its budget without a referendum.[17]

An archetypal example of a state's creation of a public authority to extricate itself from fiscal difficulties occurred in Louisiana in

1987, when the legislature established a special district, named the Louisiana Recovery District, with authority to impose a one-cent sales tax, and to issue $1.3 billion in bonds backed by the sales tax, to enable the state to pay off its accumulated operating deficit. Although the state constitution required voter approval for state debt and for both a local sales tax and local debt, the Louisiana supreme court dismissed all legal challenges to the recovery district. The district, defined by the legislature as a "special district and a political subdivision, having boundaries coterminous with the state," was not part of the state and not a local government, and thus neither its taxing nor its borrowing decisions were subject to constitutional restrictions.[18] In the words of one Louisiana legal scholar, it was "nothing more than a straw man created by the Legislature and the Governor precisely for the purpose of evading" the constitutional requirement that "the state pay its current expenses out of its current revenues."[19]

Finally, the history of state debt limitations, especially the use of nonguaranteed debt and public authority debt to circumvent restrictions, illustrates the significant and highly varied role that state courts play when state finances are subject to constitutional regulation. Court decisions, and not just the language of a state's constitution, determine the debt instruments available and the stringency of the substantive and procedural restrictions on state borrowing.

In some states, courts have effectively read debt limits out of their constitutions. The New Jersey supreme court signaled this when it called for "a degree of flexibility in methods of financing publicly needed facilities which should be accorded modern legislatures and public officials."[20] The Wisconsin supreme court recognized the tension between its state constitution's "abhorrence of public debt" and the court's endorsement of a lease-payment financing of a new high school but held: "It is not an illegal evasion of the constitution to accomplish a desired result, lawful in itself, by finding a legal way to do it."[21] The New York court of appeals dismissed the contention that "modern ingenuity, even gimmickry, have in fact stretched the words of the Constitution beyond the point of prudence" by concluding that "pleas for reform in State borrowing practices and policy" should be directed to the legislature, not the courts.[22]

Having rewritten the rules of state finance to permit legislatures to evade debt limits provided they use appropriate techniques, these courts are no longer active players in state finance. Their prior decisions, in tandem with the constitutional debt restrictions, however, have led to a restructuring of borrowing practices that affect the form and cost of debt. In other states, however, the courts have avoided giving a blank check to schemes to get around debt limits. These courts have developed doctrines that render some but not all special fund, revenue, or lease-payment bonds exempt from constitutional debt restrictions. Judicial decisions are thus necessary to determine the validity of a particular borrowing device. By relying on gossamer distinctions to differentiate those financing mechanisms that create debt in the constitutional sense from those that do not, these courts have made themselves active participants in the law and politics of public finance.

A recent study of state debt limitation cases found that "by keeping legal doctrine fluid, state courts have assured themselves a 'seat at the table' when a state contemplates a new financing scheme."[23] Kentucky courts "have developed doctrinal rules flexible enough to permit judicial re-evaluation of the legislature's original decision" to borrow. As a result Kentucky's constitutional provisions "do not operate to prohibit state debt; instead, they operate to assure a [judicial] second look at the decision to incur debt."[24] Similarly, the Illinois supreme court "has demonstrated a capacity to reach any conclusion it wants about the constitutionality of any particular financing scheme."[25] The Virginia supreme court has adopted doctrines that "effectively [allow it] . . . to substitute its judgment for that of the state legislature."[26] The Florida supreme court reviews certain types of bond issues on a project by project basis, thus assuring itself considerable "discretion to invalidate state spending decisions."[27]

Judges on many state courts "behave as if they can separate good debt from bad."[28] Moreover, "politics has almost certainly played an important—although unquantifiable—role in constitutional debt decisions."[29] In states like Kentucky or Florida, debt restrictions may have more bite than where courts generally accept legislative evasions, but the real effect of the restrictions is to vest in courts "broad discretion to review legislative debt schemes."[30]

In summary, state constitutional debt restrictions have been circumvented by new and creative financing devices that tend to drive up the costs of borrowing, encourage the fragmentation of state governments, and facilitate the evasion of balanced budget requirements. State courts have either acquiesced in evasive state borrowing techniques or built up their own role in fiscal decision-making, but they have not strictly enforced the constitutional restrictions.

The state experience provides a warning that the consequence of a federal balanced budget amendment would be not just to constrain the executive and the legislature but also to shift political power from the elected branches of government to the courts, with judicial preferences playing a role in the fiscal policymaking process. The critical provisions of the Balanced Budget Amendment passed by the House of Representatives in January 1995 are:

Section 1. Total outlays for any fiscal year shall not exceed total receipts for that fiscal year, unless three-fifths of the whole number of each House of Congress shall provide by law for a specific excess of outlays over receipts by a roll-call vote.

Section 2. The limit on the debt of the United States held by the public shall not be increased, unless three-fifths of the whole number of each House shall provide by law for such an increase by a rollcall vote.

Section 6. The Congress shall enforce and implement this article by appropriate legislation, which may rely on estimates of outlays and receipts.

Section 7. Total receipts shall include all receipts of the United States Government except those derived from borrowing. Total outlays shall include all outlays of the United States Government except for those for repayment of debt principal.[31]

Section one requires the federal budget to be balanced on a cash accounting basis unless a deficit is approved by a supermajority congressional vote. The three-fifths requirement might be avoided by borrowing the funds needed to close the gap between tax-based receipts and outlays. However, sections two and seven close that loophole by limiting the ability to incur debt without a supermajority vote, and by declaring that receipts derived from borrowing shall not be counted as receipts for budget purposes. None of these sections, though, define "the debt of the United States" or "receipts of the United States."

At the state level, the primary techniques for avoiding debt limitations have been the creation of obligations that are not treated as "debt" because they do not carry the full faith and credit of the states and the creation of quasi-autonomous public authorities, public benefit corporations, and similar entities that perform public functions but whose liabilities are not treated as debts of the states. As previously noted, Congress and the president have already chartered more than forty quasi-autonomous corporations—Amtrak, Comsat, Conrail, Fannie Mae, Sallie Mae, the Legal Services Corporation, TVA, and the entities created as part of the savings and loan bailout, among others. "While toiling in obscurity, they manage communication satellites, museums, railroads, and power generation. They provide specialized credit and insurance for housing and agriculture."[32] Some of these corporations are wholly owned by the federal government, which appoints all the directors and holds all the shares. Some have mixed public-private control, with the government owning some or none of the equity and appointing only a minority of the directors.[33] Many of these federal government corporations are already "off-budget" for spending limitation and deficit reduction purposes.[34]

Following the example of the states, Congress could: transfer existing federal spending responsibilities to some of these entities (or create additional corporations); authorize them to borrow, or enlarge existing borrowing authorizations; and, pursuant to section six of the proposed Balanced Budget Amendment, declare that the debts of these entities are not "debts of the United States." The United States would then "balance" its budget; but the dozens of quasi-autonomous federal government corporations would be running multibillion-dollar deficits. Currently, these corporations raise billions of dollars in the credit markets. Although little of their debt carries a formal federal full-faith-and-credit guarantee, most of them benefit from "an implicit guarantee"—the belief in the capital markets that the United States will back up these obligations should the need arise.[35] Relying on that implicit guarantee, the United States could expand the role of these entities in financing core federal functions. Should the implicit guarantee of the United States not be sufficient, the federal government could take a leaf from the book of the states and pledge, by statute, its moral obligation to come to the rescue of a corporation should it run into financial difficulty—taking care first to use its section six power to declare that the moral obligation is not a federal government "outlay."

Not only could borrowing be spun off to autonomous corporations whose obligations are not the "debt" of the United States, but, following the "backdoor financing" model established in New York, the proceeds of these corporate borrowings could be funneled back to the United States Treasury. Federal officials could sell assets to these entities—either disposing of them outright or selling them and leasing them back for an annual rental—with these independent entities borrowing the money to purchase the assets. If Congress used its power under section six of the Balanced Budget Amendment to draft the proper legislation, the corporation's borrowing would not be limited by section two, and the federal government's receipts would not be receipts from borrowing (precluded from counting against outlays by section seven) but income from the sale of assets properly counted as receipts under section one.

It is impossible to predict how federal courts would apply the Balanced Budget Amendment to such evasive techniques. The Supreme Court recently held that Amtrak "is an agency or instrumentality of the United States for the purpose of individual rights guaranteed against the Government by the Constitution," even though Congress by statute had declared Amtrak "not to be an agency or establishment of the United States."[36] The Amtrak decision, however, involved a question of First Amendment rights—Amtrak's content-based rejection of an artist's lease of billboard space in New York City's Pennsylvania Station. The Court expressed concern that government not be allowed "to evade the most solemn obligations imposed in the Constitution by simply resorting to the corporate form."[37] But in the absence of any experience with federal constitutional budgetary provisions, it cannot be assumed that the Court would treat the requirements of the Balanced Budget Amendment as "the most solemn obligations."

Indeed, the experience at the state level with comparable constitutional restraints has been quite the opposite.

Moreover, Amtrak is unusual in that the federal government holds all the corporation's stock and names all the directors. The Supreme Court placed great weight on the government's direct domination of Amtrak in determining that the rail passenger corporation ought to be treated as an instrumentality of the United States for First Amendment purposes. The Court expressly distinguished Amtrak from entities like Comsat and Conrail, in which the government lacked permanent voting control.[38] The Amtrak decision therefore might lead Congress and the president to increase the use of corporations in which the federal government has only a minority interest in order to avoid the strictures of the Balanced Budget Amendment. Like the states, the federal government would have to trade off the benefits of avoiding balanced budget limitations with the costs associated with loss of formal control by elected officials that would result from spinning off federal functions to mixed-ownership corporations. No doubt the president or Congress would be able to develop informal techniques for influencing, if not controlling, these bodies. Yet one consequence of relying on quasi-autonomous corporations is, inevitably, reduced accountability to the general public.

It is far from certain that anything like this scenario of evasion would develop should the Balanced Budget Amendment be ratified. The federal government corporations may not be able to take on the same role that the state public authorities have, and the federal courts may be more protective of the principles of budgetary balance and borrowing restraint than the state courts have been.

But at the very least the state experience with constitutional debt restrictions cautions against an easy optimism that courts will enforce the amendment against the president and Congress. It raises the possibility that courts will assent to legal arguments in support of accounting gimmicks that balance the budget in form but not in substance. As in the case of debt limits, a balanced budget requirement could serve, perversely, as a stimulus to off-budget spending and could shift fiscal activity and policymaking from elected officials directly accountable to the voters to the political netherworld of quasi-autonomous corporations and authorities.

Chapter 5

DO CONSTITUTIONAL BALANCED BUDGET REQUIREMENTS LEAD TO BALANCED BUDGETS?

M ost states balance their operating budgets most of the time. Although the analysis of state budgets presented here relies on the states' own numbers—which may be subject to a little manipulation—it seems that during the two decades from 1968 through 1987, the states in the aggregate balanced their operating budgets in all but two of those years.[1] A significant number of state budgets were out of balance during the recession at the beginning of the 1990s, but most returned to balance by 1993. Balance was at times precarious, dependent on accounting tricks, transfers from special funds, and the occasional surreptitious shift of operating expenses to the capital budget. But states generally kept expenditures for current programs reasonably close to matching regularly recurring revenues, and took steps to cut spending or raise taxes when deficits occurred. Although state debts have grown steadily, they are, in total, only about one-tenth of the federal debt.[2]

It is, however, doubtful that constitutional balanced budget provisions are doing the work of forcing states to bring expenditures into line with revenues. Balanced budget requirements are only a single strand in the extensive web of state constitutional regulation of state finances. As mentioned in Chapter 3, forty-three state constitutions give their governors line-item veto authority over appropriations bills, and ten of those states give their governors item-reduction authority. Most state constitutions regulate borrowing. Twenty-four states are required to deposit a portion of state revenues into "rainy day funds," that is, special funds that may be drawn upon in the event of an economic downturn.[3]

Twenty state constitutions impose some limit on state spending or state taxation.[4] They typically limit spending to a percentage of total personal income in the state, or limit the rate of spending or revenue increase to the rate of growth of the state economy or of state population. At least nine states impose a special procedural hurdle before the state may adopt a tax increase—either a supermajority in the legislature or the approval of the voters in a referendum.[5] Six states require a legislative supermajority simply for the adoption of the budget. Many states constitutionalize the process of budget adoption and include numerous detailed requirements concerning spending. Indeed, University of California-San Diego political scientist Matthew McCubbins recently determined there are "at least 170 sections in the various articles of the California Constitution that affect government budget policy."[6]

It is difficult to discern the distinct effect of a balanced budget requirement amid this welter of legal regulation of state finances. The difficulty is compounded when other fiscal rules, such as the executive budget and the governor's authority to reduce spending during the fiscal year, are thrown into the mix. W. Mark Crain and James C. Miller III, the director of the federal Office of Management and Budget in President Ronald Reagan's second term, undertook a statistical analysis of the relationship of a variety of state budget procedures to state spending growth and found that the impact of constitutional balanced budget requirements was "interdependent with [those of] the other budgetary practices."[7] They concluded that in the thirty-three states using the executive budget system, a balanced budget requirement had no independent effect on the rate of state spending growth. It did appear to slow spending in the remaining states, but it had less impact than did other variables such as the level of detail in a state's budget bills or even the number of budget bills a state typically enacted. Overall, the presence or absence of a balanced budget requirement in a state's constitution had less influence on spending growth than whether or not it used the executive budget system. Unfortunately, Crain and Miller examined only the rate of spending as an outcome, not fiscal balance.

Over the past decade several economists, political scientists, and public finance specialists have conducted statistical examinations of state legal requirements to see whether they actually constrain state spending, taxing, or borrowing. They have found that economic, political, institutional, and cultural factors are generally more significant than constitutional constraints in shaping taxing, spending, and borrowing decisions by individual states. Under some circumstances, these constitutional requirements do interact with economic and political forces, but there is little evidence that they have any real impact on their own.

Crain and Miller, for example, found that the line-item veto had little effect on state spending. Economists Burton Abrams and William Dougan reached the same result.[8] Economist Dale G. Bails studied state tax and expenditure limitations and found that "they resulted in virtually no success in limiting growth in their budgets."[9] Abrams and Dougan seconded this conclusion. Moreover, two different studies found that states with constitutional tax and expenditure limitations actually had slightly higher levels of debt.[10]

More generally, Abrams and Dougan found that constitutional limits on debt, as well as those on taxation and expenditures, and the line-item veto had no significant independent effect on state spending. Rather, they found that the most significant institutional variable to affect state spending was not any of the fiscal provisions of a state's constitution but whether the state's constitution limited the number of terms a governor could serve. Apparently, strong governors are more likely to hold down state spending, and term limits undercut gubernatorial political power.

David Nice of Washington State University found that both state balanced budget requirements and debt limits were "essentially unrelated" to state and local debt per capita or to the growth in state debt per capita. State debt limits were associated with lower full-faith-and-credit debt but had no effect on nonguaranteed debt or on total debt.

Although Roy Bahl and William Duncombe found that stringent state debt limits were associated with lower levels of nonguaranteed debt as well as lower total debt, they suggested that result might be due to "a general antidebt climate in some states that discourages all forms of debt"[11] rather than to the debt limits themselves. Nice also found a relationship between debt level and the dominant ideology in a state, with politically liberal states for the most part having higher levels of debt.[12] In general, Bahl and Duncombe found that the principal determinants of interstate differences in debt burdens were economics, demography, and history—not legal principles. States with high levels of school enrollment, high levels of water consumption, greater population density, and greater population growth rates had heavier debt burdens. Similarly, states with higher levels of debt in the past had higher current debt.[13]

In an extensive statistical study of state government indebtedness from 1961 through 1989, Texas political scientists James Clingermayer and Dan Wood confirmed that state debt is primarily a function of economic conditions reflecting both the need to borrow and the capacity to repay debt rather than legal considerations. States with greater per capita revenues also had greater per capita debts.[14] States were more likely to borrow when their growth rates declined, as governments turned to debt to finance ongoing expenditure programs. State-specific political culture also affected debt levels, with liberal states taking on higher levels of debt per capita than conservative states. The presence or absence of constitutional limits on state debt did not affect the rate of growth of borrowing.[15]

Several studies have examined the effect of balanced budget requirements on states' responses to deficits. In a review of state fiscal behavior in the early 1980s, the United States Advisory Commission on Intergovernmental Relations (ACIR), which has called for a federal balanced budget amendment, concluded that states with stringent balanced budget requirements—taking constitutional and statutory mandates together—were more likely to close budget deficits within the fiscal period in which they emerged, and that over a five-year period tough balanced budget rules were associated with smaller deficits. But even ACIR acknowledged that "the relative stringency of state balanced budget requirements was not the only apparent factor in explaining fiscal behavior, nor was it the most important. Generally, the level of state wealth (as measured by state per capita income) was a more important determinant of differences in fiscal behavior."

Two particularly subtle investigations published in 1994 indicate that the effect of balanced budget provisions is substantially dependent on political circumstances. Focusing on the reactions of the states to the unexpected fiscal downturn—and the resulting revenue shortfalls—at the start of the 1990s, James Poterba of MIT found balanced budget requirements affected states in which the governorship and the legislature were held by the same political party but had little impact in politically divided states. Poterba found that single-party states with stringent antideficit rules moved more quickly to restore budgetary balance after a fiscal shock than did single-party states without them. But in states with politically divided government, the presence or absence of antideficit rules had no relationship to how quickly they reacted to fiscal shocks.[16]

In an empirical analysis of data covering the period from 1968 to 1987, James Alt of Harvard and Robert Lowry of Michigan State reached a very similar conclusion: the presence or absence of legal limitations on the ability of states to carry over deficits into future fiscal periods had no effect on how split legislatures responded to fiscal shocks, but antideficit requirements did affect politically unified legislatures.[17] Prohibitions on the carryover of deficits actually work "only for unified governments." According to Alt and Lowry, "it seems likely that the ability to blame one party for undesirable outcomes is an important element in their effectiveness."[18]

In other words, legal balanced budget requirements per se do not compel balance. This is consistent with the absence of cases and the general lack of formal legal enforcement of balanced budget requirements. As the GAO has pointed out, "most states do not rely on formal legal sanctions to motivate balancing." State constitutions generally do not penalize governors or legislators who fail to balance the budget, nor do they typically include automatic enforcement mechanisms, such as "trigger taxes" or the sequestering of expenditures, if expenditures run ahead of or revenues fall behind forecasts.[19] State courts do not enforce constitutional balanced budget provisions against recalcitrant governors or legislatures. But when one party controls the government, an electorate sufficiently aroused about fiscal virtue can more readily determine who is to be held accountable for failure to balance the budget when a fiscal shock occurs. Over longer periods of time, though, both states with unified party government and those with split government, regardless of the presence or absence of constraints on deficits, tend to balance their budgets.[20]

If constitutional balanced budget requirements are not enforced against the states, why then do they generally balance their operating budgets? There appear to be two answers. One is political culture and tradition. A National Association of State Budget Officers survey of its members found that "for the majority of states . . . the most important factor contributing to balanced budgets is not an enforcement mechanism or a provision specifying how a shortfall will be made up. Rather it is the tradition of balancing budgets, the mindset this tradition creates, and the importance placed on balanced budgets that result in states complying with their requirements."[21] Similarly, the GAO's 1985 survey of state budget officers found that "attitude and determination, i.e., 'mind set', to maintain a balanced budget are more important than the actual legal requirement."[22] A 1993 GAO survey found that nearly as many state budget officials cited "tradition and expectation of balance" as mentioned a legal requirement (constitutional or statutory) in explaining what motivates budget balancing.

It seems likely that the real importance of a constitutional balanced budget requirement is that it signals the high value that a state's political culture sets on a balanced budget. A state with such a constitution may be more likely to balance its budget, but that is less attributable to the independent force of the legal requirement than to the political values and tradition that put it in the constitution in the first place.

The other reason states generally balance their budgets is that they have little practical alternative. States, like households or private firms, need money to pay for their expenditures. Unlike the federal government, the states cannot print their own money; the U.S. Constitution forbids it. Moreover, although the states have broad legal authority to raise revenue by taxation, their practical ability to do so is constrained by their relatively small size and open borders. All the states have a much smaller tax base than the federal government. Even California, the largest state, has an economy no more than one-eighth the size of the United States', and many states have quite tiny tax bases. Moreover, the Constitution restrains state taxation, albeit indirectly, by creating an American common market. Unlike national borders, state borders are legally porous. States cannot prohibit their residents from emigrating, nor can they bar nonresidents from competing for in-state jobs or sales. As a result, firms and households are free to move from state to state without fear that such a move will cost them access to markets in the state they have left behind. Open internal borders means that high-tax states risk the loss of their taxpayers. Indeed, a central feature of contemporary fiscal federalism is the interstate competition for jobs and taxpayers, with the resulting constraint on state taxation.

Borrowing is similarly limited, not so much by state constitutional requirements as by the interaction of the demands of credit markets with the competitive structure of the federal system. A state can borrow only when it can persuade lenders to lend at an interest rate the state can pay. Lenders will lend only if persuaded that a state has both the capacity and the will to repay according to the terms of the loan. The capacity to repay is constrained by the interstate competition that holds down taxation. If a state's current expenditures significantly outpace its current revenues, potential lenders may question whether it is capable of or committed to repaying its debts. It will be able to borrow only at a high interest rate. If the deficit is too large or too protracted, the interest rate the state faces may be prohibitive and access to capital markets may be lost altogether. Conversely, investors are likely to perceive a state with a balanced budget as a better credit risk since there is less reason to question its ability to cover operational costs and repay debts; they will loan that state money at more favorable terms.

The real fiscal discipline for the states thus comes from capital markets. Interest rates and credit ratings determine whether and how much states are able to borrow. Credit ratings reflect investors' confidence in the ability of a state to pay its debts, based in part on whether or not the state is able to achieve a rough fiscal balance in its operating budget. Such confidence may not require a budget balanced according to generally accepted accounting principles. Transitory or marginal deficits are not fatal to a state's ability to borrow, although the lenders may charge a higher interest rate. But a consistent and substantial deficit is likely to damage the state's access to credit.

Balanced budget requirements per se are not crucial, although it is possible that their presence in a constitution signals lenders that a state is committed to having sufficient revenues to repay its debts. Such a requirement may be rewarded by favorable treatment by lenders, but it is the concern about credit ratings itself, not the constraint of a constitutional requirement, that is more likely to produce a balanced budget.

Even states not subject to legal requirements that the fiscal year end in balance seek to close midyear gaps. The GAO found that in most states concern over bond ratings is a significant motivator to balance the budget. Moreover, of the ten states that took steps to eliminate deficits that emerged during the 1992 fiscal year, four were not legally bound to produce year-end balance, and one—Vermont—had no constitutional or statutory balanced budget requirement at all.[23] These states did seek to balance their budgets, but not because they were compelled to do so by constitutional mandates.

CONCLUSION

The states' experience with constitutional balanced budget requirements provides two lessons for the consideration of a federal constitutional amendment. First, the state constitutional requirements have not subjected the states to fiscal discipline. Rather, the federal Constitution and the bond market discipline state budgetary practices. Moreover, there is less to state constitutional stringency than meets the eye. Fewer states have constitutional balanced budget mandates than amendment proponents assume. Many constitutional provisions are relatively weak, and significant portions of state budgets are frequently exempted from their coverage. There is no evidence that these provisions have served as a sword, forcing recalcitrant states to bring their budgets into balance. Yet, by and large, most states, regardless of the presence or absence of constitutional requirements, balance their operating budgets most of the time. State deficits, when they occur, are relatively small and usually transitory.

States balance their budgets not because of their constitutions but because they have little practical alternative. The fiscal position of the states is enormously different from that of the federal government. The states are far more constrained—by interstate competition and the demands of the bond market—in their ability to raise money. A constitutional requirement may signal a state's commitment to fiscal balance, and states with such requirements may move more quickly to close budget gaps when they emerge. But politics and economic concerns are the real source of fiscal discipline at the state level. In the absence of comparable constraints operating at the national level, it is unlikely that a constitutional amendment would supply much discipline. More precisely, there is nothing in the state experience that demonstrates that constitutional limitations alone, unaccompanied by economic limits on the ability to tax and borrow, will compel budgetary balance.

Second, although state constitutions per se do not compel budgetary balance, their relevant provisions can affect the distribution of powers within a government, and, indeed, the very structure of the government itself. State balanced budget requirements, typically, have been accompanied by a considerable empowerment of the executive branch, with governors playing a far greater role in the submission, enactment, and implementation of state budgets than the president does at the national level. Balanced budget mandates themselves have generated little case law, but the budgetary provisions of state constitutions have given state courts a role in fiscal policymaking. Constitutionalizing rules on federal taxing and spending can only open the door to federal judicial participation in national fiscal decisionmaking.

Moreover, as the history of state debt limits suggests, a constitutional requirement can have unintended consequences, generating evasive maneuvers that perversely subvert its goals. State constitutional debt limits have promoted the growth of nonguaranteed debt and the proliferation of public authorities. Similarly, a federal balanced budget amendment would create an incentive to increase the use of fiscal gimmicks, special funds, off-budget expenditures, and quasi-autonomous entities. Many of these devices are already deployed to meet the statutory deficit reduction requirements currently on the books. The budget subject to constitutional restriction might be balanced, but that budget would probably be just a fraction of the true federal budget. Over time, more and more federal activity would probably occur outside the constitutional "budget." Underlying the call for a federal balanced budget amendment is the concern that government is "out of control" and that placing balanced budget principles in the Constitution will better enable citizens to control their government. But if the implementation of a balanced budget amendment were to track the states' experience with debt limitations, then the federal government would probably become less politically accountable, with more power shifted to unelected officials and to entities beyond the direct influence of the voters—and the budget still would not be balanced.

Thus, the state experience provides little support for a federal balanced budget constitutional amendment. State constitutional requirements do not create fiscal balance, but they do affect the structure and function of governments in ways that balanced budget advocates probably do not anticipate and almost certainly would not desire.

Notes

Introduction

1. Remarks at annual dinner of the Conservative Political Action Conference, March 1, 1985, *Public Papers of the Presidents of the United States, 1985, Book I: Ronald Reagan*, p. 228.

2. "Address to the Nation on the Iran Arms and *Contra* Aid Controversy and Administration Goals," August 12, 1987, *Public Papers of the Presidents of the United States, 1987, Book II: Ronald Reagan*, p. 944.

3. "Address to the Nation on the Balanced Budget Amendment," June 10, 1992, *Public Papers of the Presidents of the United States, 1992–93, Book I: George Bush*, p. 917.

4. The amendment would have lost by just a single vote, but Senator Dole, seeing that it would fail, switched his vote for procedural reasons.

5. Proponents have also sought to advance the balanced budget amendment through the other procedure the Constitution provides: Two-thirds of the states can call a constitutional convention that can submit an amendment directly to the states for ratification. Legislatures in thirty-two states—just two shy of the thirty-four the Constitution requires—have passed the resolutions for doing an end run around Congress and adopting a balanced budget amendment on their own via such a convention.

6. See, for example, "Note: Fiscal Policy Reform: The Ramifications of a Federal Line-Item Veto Authority and a Balanced Budget Requirement on the Budget Process," *Journal of Law and Politics* 8, no. 2 (Winter 1992): 405, 417. ("Forty-eight states already have a balanced budget requirement in their constitutions, and this fiscal policy tool has given these states substantial control over their expenditures.")

7. See Neal Devins, "A Symbolic Balanced Budget Amendment," *Journal of Law and Politics* 9, no. 1 (Fall 1992): 61, 80. ("Amendment

boosters argue that state experiences support a federal balanced budget amendment.")

8. United States General Accounting Office, briefing report to the chairman, Task Force on the Budget Process, Committee on the Budget, U.S. House of Representatives, "Budget Issues: State Balanced Budget Practices," GAO/AFMD-86-22BR, December 1985, p. 33.

CHAPTER 1

1. Ronald Snell, "Do State Balanced Budgets Really Happen?" *State Legislative Report* (National Conference of State Legislatures, Denver) 18, no. 6 (April 1993).

2. U.S. Congress, Senate, Judiciary Committee, hearing before the Subcommittee on the Constitution, 100th Cong., 2d sess., March 23, 1988, p. 57.

3. Snell, "Do State Balanced Budgets Really Happen?"

4. Ibid.

5. National Association of State Budget Officers, *State Balanced Budget Requirements: Provisions and Practice* (Washington, D.C.: National Association of State Budget Officers, June 24, 1992), p. 3.

6. Massachusetts Constitution, Art. LXIII, §2.

7. California Constitution, Art. IV, §12; Michigan Constitution, Art. V. §18; New York Constitution, Art. VII, §2.

8. National Association of State Budget Officers, *Budget Processes in the States* (Washington, D.C.: National Association of State Budget Officers, February 1995). Thirty-nine states require their legislatures to pass balanced budgets, but in eight of those states the requirement is statutory.

9. Florida Constitution, Art. VII, §1(d).

10. Colorado Constitution, Art. X, §2. The Kentucky constitution contains a virtually identical provision (Kentucky Constitution, §171).

11. Connecticut Constitution, Art. Third, §18a.

12. National Association of State Budget Officers, *State Balanced Budget Requirements*.

13. Wisconsin Constitution, Art. VIII, §5.

14. Nevada Constitution, Art. 9, §2.

15. According to NASBO, the states permitted to carry over deficits are: Arizona, California, Colorado, Illinois, Maryland, Massachusetts, Michigan, New Hampshire, New York, Pennsylvania, Texas, Vermont, and Wisconsin. With the exception of New Hampshire and Vermont these are all ordinarily considered to be balanced budget states.

16. Alabama, Arkansas, Connecticut, Iowa, Mississippi, Nevada, and Washington.

17. California, Connecticut, Delaware, Illinois, Iowa, Nebraska, New Hampshire, Pennsylvania, Texas, and Vermont.

18. Arizona, Georgia, Louisiana, Maryland, Massachusetts, Michigan, New York, Utah, Virginia, Washington, and Wisconsin.

19. That state was Nevada. According to the NASBO study, Nevada's only restriction on carrying over a deficit is statutory.

20. United States General Accounting Office, briefing report to the chairman, Committee on the Budget, House of Representatives, "Balanced Budget Requirements: State Experiences and Implications for the Federal Government," GAO/AFMD-93-58BR, March 1993, p. 3; Donald W. Kiefer, William A. Cox, and Dennis Zimmerman, "A Balanced Budget Constitutional Amendment: Economic Issues," Congressional Research Service report CRS 92-4585, May 26, 1992, p. 23.

21. Ibid.

22. National Association of State Budget Officers, *State Balanced Budget Requirements*, p. 1.

23. United States General Accounting Office, briefing report to the chairman, Task Force on the Budget Process, Committee on the Budget, U.S. House of Representatives, "Budget Issues: State Balanced Budget Practices," GAO/AFMD-86-22BR, December 1985, p. 30.

24. National Association of State Budget Officers, *State Balanced Budget Requirements*, p. 1.

25. United States General Accounting Office, "Balanced Budget Requirements," p. 19.

CHAPTER 2

1. National Association of State Budget Officers, *Budget Processes in the States* (Washington, D.C.: National Association of State Budget Officers, February 1995), p. 5.

2. United States General Accounting Office, briefing report to the chairman, Task Force on the Budget Process, Committee on the Budget, U.S. House of Representatives, "Budget Issues: State Balanced Budget Practices," GAO/AFMD-86-22BR, December 1985, p. 33.

3. Ibid.

4. Jeffrey I. Chapman, "California: The Enduring Crisis," in Steven D. Gold, ed., *The Fiscal Crisis of the States: Lessons for the Future* (Washington, D.C.: Georgetown University Press, 1995), p. 108.

5. Ibid., p. 115.

6. Ibid., p. 108.

7. Ibid., p. 122.

8. Ibid., p. 108; *State Budget & Tax News* 13, no. 23 (December 5, 1994): 6.

9. United States General Accounting Office, "Budget Issues," p. 62.

10. Kevin S. Rosenberg, "Enacting the California State Budget: Two-Thirds Is Too Much," 25 *Pacific Law Journal* 67, 69 (1993).

11. Citizens Budget Commission, "Guiding Principles for Changing Times," discussion paper prepared for the commission's Budget 2000 Conference, Palisades, N.Y., May 12–13, 1995, p. 4.

12. Carol W. Lewis, "Connecticut: Surviving Tax Reform," in Gold, *Fiscal Crisis of the States*, pp. 152–54.

13. Bruce A. Wallin, "Massachusetts: Downsizing Government," in ibid., p. 255.

14. Ibid., p. 267.

15. See Robert J. Kleine, "Michigan: Rethinking Fiscal Priorities," in ibid., p. 306. ($310 million fiscal year 1990 deficit carried over into fiscal year 1991.)

16. Thomas F. Luce, Jr., "Minnesota: Innovation in an Era of Constraint," in ibid., p. 359. (Minnesota engaged in deficit spending in five of the first six fiscal years of the 1990s, although the deficits were covered, in part, by the state's ample reserves.)

17. Kleine, "Michigan: Rethinking Fiscal Priorities," p. 296.

18. Council of State Governments, *The Book of the States, 1994–95* (Lexington, Ky.: Council of State Governments, 1994), pp. 338–39, Tables 6.8, 6.9. Aggregate state revenues exceeded aggregate expenditures only when trust funds were factored in. For most trust funds, especially pension funds, current revenues greatly exceed current expenditures since these funds are operated on an actuarial rather than a pay-as-you-go basis, with today's revenues invested to generate the funds that will pay future pensions and today's expenditures financed by earlier revenues placed in the funds and the investment income those revenues have earned.

19. Ibid.

20. *State Budget & Tax News* 13, no. 23 (December 5, 1994): 7.

21. H. Carl McCall, "Fiscal Review of the Enacted 1995–96 Budget," Office of the Comptroller, State of New York, Albany, July 1995, pp. 8–12. Spending estimates were reduced by $389 million; revenue estimates were increased by $335 million.

22. See Harold Wolman and George Peterson, "State and Local Government Strategies for Responding to Fiscal Pressure," 55 *Tulane Law Review* 773 (1981) (discussion of optimistic budgeting).

23. Ibid.

24. Thus, Minnesota accelerated income tax withholding and required early recognition of property taxes, and New York and California moved forward the dates for payment of income and sales taxes. See United

States General Accounting Office, "Budget Issues," pp. 64, 76; McCall, "Fiscal Review of the Enacted 1995–96 Budget," pp. 26–27.

25. United States General Accounting Office, "Budget Issues," p. 72.

26. McCall, "Fiscal Review of the Enacted 1995–96 Budget," p. 11.

27. Wallin, "Massachusetts: Downsizing Government," p. 256.

28. See Condell v. Bress, 983 F.2d 415 (2d Cir. 1993); Association of Surrogates and Supreme Court Reporters v. State, 940 F.2d 766 (2d Cir. 1991); Association of Surrogates and Supreme Court Reporters v. State, 79 N.Y.2d 39 (1992). See also Opinion of the Justices, 609 A.2d 1204 (S.Ct. N.H. 1992) (holding that a bill requiring certain New Hampshire state employees to take unpaid leave would violate collective bargaining agreement and would be substantial impairment of contractual rights not justified by state budget problems).

29. Chiles v. United Faculty of Florida, 615 So.2d 671 (S.Ct. Fla. 1993).

30. Massachusetts Community College Council v. Commonwealth, 649 NE2d 708 (S.J.C. Mass. 1995).

31. Kleine, "Michigan: Rethinking Fiscal Priorities," p. 307.

32. Musselman v. Governor, 533 NW2d 237, 241 (S.Ct. Mich. 1995).

33. Dadisman v. Moore 384 SE2d 816, 828 (W.Va. 1988).

34. Valdes v. Cory, 189 Cal. Rptr. 212, 224 (Ct.App. 1983).

35. McDermott v. Regan, 82 N.Y.2d 354, 361 (1993).

36. *State Budget & Tax News* 13, no. 14 (June 30, 1994): 12.

37. People ex rel Sklodowski v. State, 642 NE2d 1180, 1189 (Ill. 1994) (Freeman, J., concurring and dissenting).

38. *State Budget & Tax News* 12, no. 10 (May 4, 1993): 7.

39. Wolman and Peterson, "State and Local Government Strategies for Responding to Fiscal Pressure" (noting that over a five-year period Alabama "routinely" delayed payment for services performed under Medicaid until the next fiscal year).

40. McCall, "Fiscal Review of the Enacted 1995–96 Budget," p. 17.

41. Citizens Budget Commission, "Guiding Principles for Changing Times," p. 7.

42. McCall, "Fiscal Review of the Enacted 1995–96 Budget," pp. 27–28.

43. United States General Accounting Office, "Budget Issues," p. 64.

44. Susan A. MacManus, "Florida: Reinvention Derailed," in Gold, *Fiscal Crisis of the States*, pp. 227–28.

45. See, e.g., State Compensation Fund v. Symington, 848 P.2d 273 (Ariz. 1993); Contractors Association of West Virginia v. West Virginia Department of Public Safety, 434 SE2d 357 (W.Va. 1993).

46. McCall, "Fiscal Review of the Enacted 1995–96 Budget," p. 26.

47. Chapman, "California: The Enduring Crisis," pp. 113–14, 119.

48. United States General Accounting Office, briefing report to the

chairman, Committee on the Budget, U.S. House of Representatives, "Balanced Budget Requirements: State Experiences and Implications for the Federal Government," GAO/AFMD-93-58BR, March 1993, pp. 25–36.

49. Ron Snell, ed., *Financing State Government in the 1990s* (Denver: National Conference of State Legislatures, December 1993), p. 5.

50. The Budget Enforcement Act of 1990 officially used the term "off-budget" in declaring that the receipts and disbursements of the Federal Old-Age and Survivors Insurance Trust Fund and the Federal Disability Insurance Trust Fund "shall not be counted as new budget authority, outlays, receipts, or deficit or surplus" for purposes of calculating the budget for the application of other deficit control legislation. Pub. L. 101–508, sec. 13301.

51. See Pub. L. 99–177, sec. 255, 99 Stat. 1082–86. The most prominent program on the list is Social Security.

52. Pub. L. 100–119, sec. 104, 101 Stat. 775–777.

53. Stanley E. Collender, *The Guide to the Federal Budget: Fiscal 1993* (Washington, D.C.: Urban Institute Press, 1992), p. 12.

54. See A. Michael Froomkin, "Reinventing the Government Corporation," 1995 *University of Illinois Law Review* 543, 549 (1995).

55. Ibid., p. 559.

56. Ibid., p. 615, nn. 367–69.

57. Ibid., p. 558, n. 79; see also ibid., pp. 559, 614–18.

58. For other instances of federal fiscal manipulation to meet statutory deficit reduction requirements, see Kate Stith, "Rewriting the Fiscal Constitution: The Case of Gramm-Rudman-Hollings," 76 *California Law Review* 593, 637–38 (1988) (manipulation of outlay estimates to meet Gramm-Rudman-Hollings requirements; use of asset sales that reduce "the annual cash-flow deficit but also eliminat[e] the future income from these assets").

59. United States Advisory Commission on Intergovernmental Relations, *Significant Features of Fiscal Federalism 1994*, Washington, D.C., December 1994, p. 8, Table B. In 1992, total state expenditures were $702 billion, of which grants to local governments accounted for $202 billion.

60. Snell, *Financing State Government in the 1990s*, p. 10.

61. Michigan Association of Counties v. Department of Management and Budget, 345 NW2d 584, 592 (Mich. 1984).

62. West Virginia Education Association v. Legislature, 369 SE2d 454 (S.Ct. W.Va. 1988).

63. Durant v. Department of Education, 463 NW2d 461, 476 (Mich. App. 1989) ("a specific level of categorical aid is established by constitutional mandate. . . . Therefore, categorical aid is exempt from executive order reduction. . . . [W]hile the Governor may not reduce the level

of categorical aid . . . the governor may reduce appropriations for unrestricted school aid").

64. Gold, *Fiscal Crisis of the States*, p. 33.

65. Ibid., p. 173.

66. Ibid., p. 266.

67. California's manipulation of the state-local relationship during the state fiscal crisis at the start of the decade was particularly complex. Because of a state constitutional provision guaranteeing public schools 40 percent of all new state revenues, tax increases were of limited benefit to the state. Thus, it reallocated a portion of the property tax that had hitherto been used for the general support of local governments to the schools. In addition, the state reduced its support for a range of social services, as well as mental health and indigent health care programs, in effect transferring greater fiscal responsibility for these programs to localities. To offset the loss of property tax revenues and the increased service burden, the state allowed localities to impose a sales tax surcharge and allocated to localities the proceeds of certain fees. In theory, localities benefited from greater administrative discretion in the operations of these programs, some relaxation in state mandates, and the greater reliability of the new local taxes as opposed to the inherent uncertainty of state appropriations. Nevertheless, the affected localities still have less revenue available for their programs than before the state cutbacks.

68. Gold, *Fiscal Crisis of the States*, p. 380.

69. Ibid., p. 110.

70. Ibid., p. 305.

71. Ibid., pp. 144, 152.

72. See Kenneth J. Drexler, "The Four Causes of the State and Local Budget Crisis and Proposed Solutions," *Urban Lawyer* 26, no. 3 (Summer 1994): 563, 576–77, 582.

73. Gold, *Fiscal Crisis of the States*, pp. 28–31.

74. United States Advisory Commission on Intergovernmental Relations, *Significant Features of Fiscal Federalism*, p. 180, Table 96.

75. Ibid., p. 181, Table 97.

76. Wolman and Peterson, "State and Local Government Strategies for Responding to Fiscal Pressure," pp. 783–86.

CHAPTER 3

1. Missouri Constitution, Art. IV, §27.

2. State ex rel Sikeston R-VI School District v. Ashcroft, 828 SW2d 372 (Mo. 1992).

3. North Carolina Constitution, Art. III, §5(3). Emphasis by author.

4. Council of State Governments, *The Book of the States, 1994–95* (Lexington, Ky.: Council of State Governments, 1994), p. 42.

5. United States General Accounting Office, briefing report to the chairman, Committee on the Budget, U.S. House of Representatives, "Balanced Budget Requirements: State Experiences and Implications for the Federal Government," GAO/AFMD-93-58BR, March 1993, p. 22.

6. Florida Constitution, Art. IV, §13.

7. Dodak v. State Administrative Board, 495 NW2d 539 (Mich. 1993).

8. Indexing is the recalibrating of tax brackets to take account of inflation, in order to prevent "bracket creep"—the phenomenon common to progressive tax systems in which inflation pushes people into higher tax brackets even though their real incomes have not increased.

9. United States General Accounting Office, briefing report to the chairman, Task Force on the Budget Process, Committee on the Budget, U.S. House of Representatives, "Budget Issues: State Balanced Budget Practices," GAO/AFMD-86-22BR, December 1985, p. 75.

10. In re State Employees' Union, 587 A.2d 919 (R.I. 1991).

11. In re Advisory Opinion to the House of Representatives, 576 A.2d 1371 (R.I. 1990).

12. County of Oneida v. Berle, 404 NE2d 133 (N.Y. 1980).

13. Opinion of the Justices, 376 NE2d 1217, 1221 (Mass. 1978).

14. Board of Education v. Gilligan, 36 Ohio App.2d 15, affirmed 38 Ohio St.2d 107 (1973); Bruneau v. Edwards, 517 So.2d 818 (La. Ct.App. 1987).

15. State v. Fairbanks North Star Borough, 736 P.2d 1140 (Alaska) 1987.

16. Fairbanks North Star Borough v. State, 753 P.2d 1158 (Alaska 1988).

17. Chiles v. Children, 589 So.2d 260 (Fla. 1991).

18. See also "Note: Fiscal Policy Reform: The Ramifications of a Federal Line-Item Veto Authority and a Balanced Budget Requirement on the Budget Process," *Journal of Law and Politics* 8, no. 2 (Winter 1992): 405.

19. Bishop v. Governor of Maryland, 380 A.2d 220 (Md. App. 1977).

20. Wein v. Carey, 41 N.Y.2d 498 (1977).

21. New York Constitution, Art. VII, §9.

22. Wein v. State, 39 N.Y.2d 136, 147–48 (1976).

23. 41 N.Y.2d 503.

24. Ibid., p. 505.

25. Ibid., p. 504.

26. Ibid.

27. Ibid., p. 505.

28. For a discussion of how these three factors might affect judicial enforcement of a federal balanced budget amendment, see "Note: Article III Problems in Enforcing the Balanced Budget Amendment," 83 *Columbia Law Review* 1065 (1983).

29. As the Illinois supreme court observed in finding that a suit brought to enjoin the transfer of monies from State Pensions Fund to the state's general revenue fund had been rendered moot by the transfer of the monies, "the judicial decisionmaking and its role in the government's balance of powers has certain defined limits." People ex rel Sklodowski v. State, 642 NE2d 1180, 1185, 1187 (Ill. 1994). Two members of the court blasted the majority for its "willingness to weigh political expediency in crafting the constitutional jurisprudence of this State" (Justices Freeman and Harrison, concurring in part and dissenting in part).

30. See, e.g., Carlstrom v. AFT, 694 P.2d 1 (Wash. 1985) (asserting independent authority to evaluate state's claim of financial emergency, and invalidating state legislative cancellation of contractual salary increases).

31. Hickel v. Cowper, 874 P.2d 922, 926 (Alaska 1994).

32. In re Advisory Opinion to the Governor—State Revenue Cap, 658 So.2d 77 (Fla. 1995).

CHAPTER 4

1. See, e.g., Indiana Constitution, Art. X, §5; West Virginia Constitution, Art. X, §4.

2. See, e.g., Arizona Constitution, Art. IX, §5 (aggregate amount of state debt shall never exceed the sum of $350,000).

3. See, e.g., Georgia Constitution, Art. III, §4, paragraph II (debt service limited to 10 percent of revenue receipts); Hawaii Constitution, Art. VII, §13 (debt service limited to 20 percent of the average of state revenues in the three fiscal years immediately preceding); Nevada Constitution, Art. IX, §3 (state debts limited to 2 percent of the assessed valuation of the state); Washington Constitution, Art. VIII, §1 (debt service on state debt limited to 9 percent of the average of state revenues in the three fiscal years immediately preceding).

4. See, e.g., Oklahoma Constitution, Art. X, §25.

5. See, e.g., California Constitution, Art. XVI, §1 (debt limited to $300,000; additional debt may be authorized by law passed by two-thirds vote of each house of legislature and approved by voters in referendum); Delaware Constitution, Art. VIII, §3 (requiring approval of three-fourths of each house of the legislature); Illinois Constitution, Art. IX, §9 (debt requires approval of either three-fifths of each house or of majority of

voters in referendum); Michigan Constitution, Art. IX, §15 (long-term borrowing requires approval of two-thirds of each house and approval by voters in referendum); Montana Constitution, Art. VIII, §8 (debt requires approval of either two-thirds of the members of each house or a majority of voters in referendum).

6. William H. Stewart, *The Alabama Constitution: A Reference Guide* (Westport, Conn.: Greenwood Press, 1994), pp. 115–16.

7. See M. David Gelfand, *State and Local Government Debt Financing* (New York: Clark Boardman Callaghan, 1992), vol. I, App. 2B.

8. Bulman v. McCrane, 312 A.2d 857 (N.J. 1973).

9. Council of State Governments, *The Book of the States, 1994–95* (Lexington, Ky.: Council of State Governments, 1994), p. 328.

10. United States Advisory Commission on Intergovernmental Relations, *Significant Features of Fiscal Federalism 1994*, Washington, D.C., December 1994, p. 164, Table 88.

11. Council of State Governments, *Book of the States,* p. 355, Table 6.18.

12. United States Advisory Commission on Intergovernmental Relations, *Significant Features of Fiscal Federalism,* pp. 168–69, Table 91.

13. See David C. Nice, "The Impact of State Policies to Limit Debt Financing," *Publius: The Journal of Federalism* 21, no. 1 (Winter 1991): 69. See also James C. Clingermayer and B. Dan Wood, "Disentangling Patterns of State Debt Financing," *American Political Science Review* 89, no. 1 (March 1995): 108.

14. Gelfand, *State and Local Government Debt Financing,* section 2.30.

15. Beverly S. Bunch, "The Effect of Constitutional Debt Limits on State Governments' Use of Public Authorities," *Public Choice* 68, no. 1 (January 1991): 57, 65.

16. Ibid.

17. See Schulz v. State, 81 N.Y.2d 336 (1993).

18. Board of Directors v. All Taxpayers, 529 So.2d 384 (La. 1988).

19. John Devlin, "Louisiana Constitutional Law," 49 *Louisiana Law Review* 395, 411 (1988).

20. Bulman v. McCrane.

21. Dierck v. Unified School District of Antigo, 477 NW2d 613 (Wis. 1991).

22. Schulz v. State, 84 N.Y.2d 231, 250 (1994).

23. Stewart E. Sterk and Elizabeth S. Goldman, "Controlling Legislative Shortsightedness: The Effectiveness of Constitutional Debt Limitations," 1991 *Wisconsin Law Review* 1301, 1333–34 (1991).

24. Ibid., pp. 1344–45.

25. Ibid., pp. 1347–48.

26. Ibid., p. 1348.

27. Ibid., p. 1357.
28. Ibid., p. 1360.
29. Ibid., p. 1359.
30. Ibid., p. 1360.
31. U.S. Congress, Joint Res. 1, 104th Cong., 1st sess., passed January 26, 1995.
32. A. Michael Froomkin, "Reinventing the Government Corporation," 1995 *University of Illinois Law Review* 547 (1995).
33. Ibid., pp. 554–55.
34. Ibid., p. 559.
35. Ibid., pp. 555, 559.
36. Lebron v. National Railroad Passenger Corporation, 115 S.Ct. 961, 972 (1995).
37. Ibid., p. 973.
38. Ibid., pp. 970, 974.

CHAPTER 5

1. See James E. Alt and Robert C. Lowry, "Divided Government, Fiscal Institutions, and Budget Deficits: Evidence from the States," *American Political Science Review* 88, no. 4 (December 1994): 811.
2. United States Advisory Commission on Intergovernmental Relations, *Significant Features of Fiscal Federalism 1994*, Washington, D.C., December 1994, p. 164, Table 88. In 1992, aggregate state debt was $371.9 billion, or 6.2 percent of GDP. The federal debt was $4,083 billion—or 67.6 percent of GDP.
3. United States Advisory Commission on Intergovernmental Relations, *Fiscal Discipline in the Federal System: National Reform and the Experience of the States*, Washington, D.C., July 1987, p. 38, Table 2.
4. Ibid. The ACIR report indicates that eighteen states have tax and expenditure limits. Since the report's publication Connecticut and Florida have also adopted limits.
5. National Association of State Budget Officers, *Budget Processes in the States*, Washington, D.C., February 1995, pp. 48–49.
6. Matthew D. McCubbins, "Putting the State Back into State Government: The Constitution and the Budget," in Bruce E. Cain and Roger G. Noll, eds., *Constitutional Reform in California: Making State Government More Effective and Responsive* (Berkeley, Calif.: IGS Press, Institute of Governmental Studies, University of California, 1995).
7. W. Mark Crain and James C. Miller III, "Budget Process and Spending Growth," 31 *William and Mary Law Review* 1021, 1042 (1990).

8. Burton A. Abrams and William R. Dougan, "The Effects of Constitutional Restraints on Governmental Spending," *Public Choice* 49, no. 2 (March 1986): 101.

9. Dale G. Bails, "The Effectiveness of Tax-Expenditure Limitations: A Re-Evaluation," *American Journal of Economics and Society* 49, no. 2 (April 1990): 223.

10. Roy Bahl and William Duncombe, "State and Local Debt Burdens in the 1980s: A Study in Contrasts," *Public Administration Review* 53, no. 1 (January/February 1993): 31, 38; James C. Clingermayer and B. Dan Wood, "Disentangling Patterns of State Debt Financing," *American Political Science Review* 89, no. 1 (March 1995): 108, 115–17.

11. Bahl and Duncombe, "State and Local Debt Burdens," p. 38.

12. David C. Nice, "The Impact of State Policies to Limit Debt Financing," *Publius: The Journal of Federalism* 21, no. 1 (Winter 1991) : 77.

13. Bahl and Duncombe, "State and Local Debt Burdens," p. 38.

14. Clingermayer and Wood, "Disentangling Patterns of State Debt Financing," pp. 116–17.

15. Ibid., p. 117.

16. James M. Poterba, "State Responses to Fiscal Crises: The Effects of Budgetary Institutions and Politics," *Journal of Political Economy* 102, no. 4 (August 1994): 799, 816–18.

17. Alt and Lowry, "Divided Government, Fiscal Institutions, and Budget Deficits."

18. Ibid.

19. United States General Accounting Office, briefing report to the chairman, Committee on the Budget, U.S. House of Representatives, "Balanced Budget Requirements: State Experiences and Implications for the Federal Government," GAO/AFMD-93-58BR (March 1993) p. 21.

20. Alt and Lowry, "Divided Government, Fiscal Institutions, and Budget Deficits," p. 822.

21. National Association of State Budget Officers, *State Balanced Budget Requirements: Provisions and Practice*, Washington, D.C., June 24, 1992, p. 3.

22. United States General Accounting Office, briefing report to the chairman, Task Force on the Budget Process, Committee on the Budget, U.S. House of Representatives, "Budget Issues: State Balanced Budget Practices," GAO/AFMD-86-22BR (December 1985), p. 46.

23. United States General Accounting Office, "Balanced Budget Requirements," p. 39.

BIBLIOGRAPHY

Abrams, Burton A., and William R. Dougan. "The Effects of Constitutional Restraints on Governmental Spending." *Public Choice*
49 (1986): 101.

Alt, James E., and Robert C. Lowry. "Divided Government, Fiscal
Institutions, and Budget Deficits: Evidence from the States."
American Political Science Review 88 (1994): 811.

Aronson, J. Richard, and John L. Hilley. *Financing State and Local
Governments.* 4th ed. Washington, D.C.: Brookings Institution, 1986.

Bahl, Roy, and William Duncombe. "State and Local Debt Burdens in
the 1980s: A Study in Contrasts." *Public Administration Review* 53
(1993): 31.

Bails, Dale G. "The Effectiveness of Tax-Expenditure Limitations: A Re-
Evaluation." *American Journal of Economics and Society* 49
(1990): 223.

Briffault, Richard. "The Item Veto in State Courts." 66 *Temple Law
Review* 1171 (1993).

Bunch, Beverly S. "The Effect of Constitutional Debt Limits on State
Governments' Use of Public Authorities." *Public Choice* 68 (1991): 57.

Cain, Bruce E., and Roger G. Noll. *Constitutional Reform in California:
Making State Government More Effective and Responsive.* Berkeley,
Calif.: IGS Press, Institute of Governmental Studies, University of
California, 1995.

Chapman, Jeffrey I. "California: The Enduring Crisis." In *The Fiscal
Crisis of the States. See* Gold 1995.

Citizens Budget Commission. *Guiding Principles for Changing Times.*
New York: Citizens Budget Commission, May 1995.

Clingermayer, James C., and B. Dan Wood. "Disentangling Patterns of State
Debt Financing." *American Political Science Review* 89 (1995): 108.

Collender, Stanley E. *The Guide to the Federal Budget: Fiscal 1993*. Washington, D.C.: Urban Institute Press, 1992.

"Comment: Enacting the California State Budget: Two-Thirds Is Too Much." 25 *Pacific Law Journal* 67 (1993).

Council of State Governments. *The Book of the States 1994–95*. Lexington, Ky.: Council of State Governments, 1994.

Crain, W. Mark, and James C. Miller. "Budget Process and Spending Growth." 31 *William and Mary Law Review* 1021 (1990).

Devins, Neal. "Budget Reform and the Balance of Power." 31 *William and Mary Law Review* 993 (1990).

_____. "A Symbolic Balanced Budget Amendment." *Journal of Law and Politics* 9 (1992): 61.

Devlin, John. "Louisiana Constitutional Law." 49 *Louisiana Law Review* 395 (1988).

Drexler, Kenneth J. "The Four Causes of the State and Local Budget Crisis and Proposed Solutions." *Urban Lawyer* 26 (1994): 563.

Froomkin, A. Michael. "Reinventing the Government Corporation." 1995 *University of Illinois Law Review* 543 (1995).

Gelfand, M. David, ed. *State and Local Government Debt Financing*. 3 vols. New York: Clark Boardman Callaghan, 1994.

Gold, Steven D., ed. *The Fiscal Crisis of the States: Lessons for the Future*. Washington, D.C.: Georgetown University Press, 1995.

Kiefer, Donald W., William A. Cox, and Dennis Zimmerman. "A Balanced Budget Constitutional Amendment: Economic Issues." Congressional Research Service report CRS 92-4585, Washington, D.C., May 26, 1992.

Kiewit, D. Roderick. "Constitutional Limitations on Indebtedness: The Case of California." In *Constitutional Reform in California*. See Cain and Noll 1995.

Kirkland, Kenneth J. "'Creative Accounting' and Short-Term Debt: State Responses to the Deficit Threat." *National Tax Journal* 36 (1983): 395.

Kleine, Robert J. "Michigan: Rethinking Fiscal Priorities." In *The Fiscal Crisis of the States. See* Gold 1995.

Luce, Thomas F., Jr. "Minnesota: Innovation in an Era of Constraint." In *The Fiscal Crisis of the States. See* Gold 1995.

MacManus, Susan A. "Florida: Reinvention Derailed." In *The Fiscal Crisis of the States. See* Gold 1995.

McCall, H. Carl. "Fiscal Review of the Enacted 1995-96 Budget." Office of the Comptroller, State of New York, Albany, July 1995.

McCubbins, Mathew D. "Putting the State Back into State Government: The Constitution and the Budget." In *Constitutional Reform in California. See* Cain and Noll 1995.

National Association of State Budget Officers. *State Balanced Budget Requirements: Provisions and Practice*. Washington, D.C.: National Association of State Budget Officers, June 24, 1992.

————. *Budget Processes in the States*. Washington, D.C.: National Association of State Budget Officers, February 1995.

National Conference of State Legislatures. "Do State Balanced Budgets Really Happen?" *State Legislative Report* 18, no. 6 (April 1993).

Nice, David C. "The Impact of State Policies to Limit Debt Financing." *Publius: The Journal of Federalism* 21 (1991): 69.

"Note: Article III Problems in Enforcing the Balanced Budget Amendment." 83 *Columbia Law Review* 1065 (1983).

"Note: Fiscal Policy Reform: The Ramifications of a Federal Line-Item Veto Authority and a Balanced Budget Requirement on the Budget Process." *Journal of Law and Politics* 8 (1992): 405, 417.

Poterba, James M. "State Responses to Fiscal Crises: The Effects of Budgetary Institutions and Politics." *Journal of Political Economy* 102 (1994): 799.

Ratchford, B. U. *American State Debts*. Durham, N.C.: Duke University Press, 1941.

Rosenberg, Kevin S. "Enacting the California State Budget: Two-Thirds Is Too Much." 25 *Pacific Law Journal* 67, 69 (1993).

Savage, James D. *Balanced Budgets and American Politics*. Ithaca, N.Y.: Cornell University Press, 1988.

Snell, Ron. "Do States Really Balance Their Budgets?" *Legisbrief* (National Conference of State Legislatures, Denver) 1, no. 6 (February 1993).

————, ed. *Financing State Government in the 1990s*. Denver: National Conference of State Legislatures, December 1993.

Sterk, Stewart E., and Elizabeth S. Goldman. "Controlling Legislative Shortsightedness: The Effectiveness of Constitutional Debt Limitations." 1991 *Wisconsin Law Review* 1301 (1991).

Stewart, William H. *The Alabama Constitution: A Reference Guide*. Westport, Conn.: Greenwood Press, 1994.

Stith, Kate. "Rewriting the Fiscal Constitution: The Case of Gramm-Rudman-Hollings." 76 *California Law Review* 593 (1988).

United States Advisory Commission on Intergovernmental Relations. *Fiscal Discipline in the Federal System: National Reform and the Experience of the States*. Washington, D.C.: United States Advisory Commission on Intergovernmental Relations, July 1987.

————. *Significant Features of Fiscal Federalism 1994*. Washington, D.C.: United States Advisory Commission on Intergovernmental Relations, December 1994.

United States General Accounting Office. Briefing report to the chair-
man, Task Force on the Budget Process, Committee on the Budget,
U.S. House of Representatives, "Budget Issues: State Balanced
Budget Practices." GAO/AFMD-86-22BR, December 1985.
_____. Briefing report to the chairman, Committee on the Budget, House
of Representatives, "Balanced Budget Requirements: State
Experiences and Implications for the Federal Government."
GAO/AFMD-93-58BR, March 1993.
Wallin, Bruce A. "Massachusetts: Downsizing Government." In *The Fiscal
Crisis of the States. See* Gold 1995.
Wolman, Harold, and George Peterson. "State and Local Government
Strategies for Responding to Fiscal Pressure." 55 *Tulane Law Review*
773 (1981).

TABLE OF CASES

Association of Surrogates and Supreme Court Reporters v. State, 940
F.2d 766 (2d Cir. 1991)

Association of Surrogates and Supreme Court Reporters v. State, 79
N.Y.2d 39 (1992)

Bishop v. Governor of Maryland, 380 A.2d 220 (Md. App. 1977)

Board of Directors v. All Taxpayers, 529 So.2d 384 (La. 1988)

Board of Education v. Gilligan, 36 Ohio App.2d 15 (1973)

Bruneau v. Edwards, 517 So.2d 818 (La. App. 1987)

Bulman v. McCrane, 312 A.2d 857 (N.J. 1973)

Carlstrom v. AFT, 694 P.2d 1 (Wash. 1985)

Chiles v. Children, 589 So.2d 260 (Fla. 1991)

Chiles v. United Faculty of Florida, 615 So.2d 671 (Fla. 1993)

Condell v. Bress, 983 F.2d 415 (2d Cir. 1993)

Contractors Association of West Virginia v. West Virginia Department
of Public Safety, 434 SE2d 357 (W.Va. 1993)

County of Oneida v. Berle, 404 NE2d 133 (N.Y. 1980)

Dadisman v. Moore, 384 SE2d 816 (W.Va. 1988)

Dierck v. Unified School District of Antigo, 477 NW2d 613 (Wis. 1991)

Dodak v. State Administrative Board, 495 NW2d 539 (Mich. 1993)

Durant v. Department of Education, 463 NW2d 461 (Mich. App. 1989)

Fairbanks North Star Borough v. State, 753 P.2d 1158 (Alaska 1988)

Hickel v. Cowper, 874 P.2d 920 (Alaska 1994)

In re Advisory Opinion to the Governor—State Revenue Cap, 658 So.2d
77 (Fla. 1995)

In re Advisory Opinion to the House of Representatives, 576 A.2d 1371 (R.I. 1990)

In re State Employees' Union, 587 A.2d 919 (R.I. 1991)

Karcher v. Kean, 479 A.2d 403 (N.J. 1984)

Lebron v. National Railroad Passenger Corporation, 115 S.Ct. 961 (1995)

Massachusetts Community College Council v. Commonwealth, 649 NE2d 708 (Mass. 1995)

McDermott v. Regan, 82 N.Y.2d 354 (1993)

Michigan Association of Counties v. Department of Management and Budget, 345 NW2d 584 (Mich. 1984)

Musselman v. Governor, 533 NW2d 237 (Mich. 1995)

Opinion of the Justices, 376 NE2d 1217 (Mass. 1978)

Opinion of the Justices, 609 A.2d 1204 (N.H. 1992)

People ex rel Sklodowski v. State, 642 NE2d 1180 (Ill. 1994)

Schulz v. State, 81 N.Y.2d 336 (1993)

Schulz v. State, 84 N.Y.2d 231 (1994)

State v. Fairbanks North Star Borough, 736 P.2d 1140 (Alaska 1987)

State Compensation Fund v. Symington, 848 P.2d 273 (Ariz. 1993)

State ex rel Sikeston R-VI School Disrict v. Ashcroft, 828 SW2d 372 (Mo. 1992)

Valdes v. Cory, 189 Cal.Rptr. 212 (Cal. App. 1983)

Wein v. Carey, 41 N.Y.2d 498 (1977)

Wein v. State, 39 N.Y.2d 136 (1976)

West Virginia Education Association v. Legislature, 369 SE2d 454 (W.Va. 1988)

Index

ABOUT THE AUTHOR

Richard Briffault is a professor of law and director of the Legislative Drafting Research Fund at Columbia University School of Law.